D0181135

A WOMAN'S GUIDE TO KNOWING WHAT YOU

HOW TO LOVE GOD WITH YOUR HEART AND YOUR MIND

PATTY HOUSER

BETHANYHOUSE

a division of Baker Publishing Group
Minneapolis, Minnesota

© 2015 by Patty Houser

Published by Bethany House Publishers
11400 Hampshire Avenue South
Bloomington, Minnesota 55438
www.bethanyhouse.com

Bethany House Publishers is a division of
Baker Publishing Group, Grand Rapids, Michigan

Printed in the United States of America

All rights reserved. No part of this publication may be reproduced, stored in a retrieval system, or transmitted in any form or by any means—for example, electronic, photocopy, recording—without the prior written permission of the publisher. The only exception is brief quotations in printed reviews.

Library of Congress Cataloging-in-Publication Data

Houser, Patty.
    A woman's guide to knowing what you believe : how to love God with your heart and your mind / Patty Houser.
        pages cm
    Includes bibliographical references.
    Summary: "A guide for Christian women to help them articulate their beliefs and share their faith. Includes questions for personal or group study"— Provided by publisher.
        ISBN 978-0-7642-1708-1 (pbk. : alk. paper)
        1. Christian women—Religious life. 2. Theology. 3. Theology, Doctrinal. I. Title.
    BV4527.H6883 2015
    248.8′43—dc23   2015015857

All Scripture quotations are from the Holy Bible, New International Version®. NIV®. Copyright © 1973, 1978, 1984, 2011 by Biblica, Inc.™ Used by permission of Zondervan. All rights reserved worldwide. www.zondervan.com

Cover design by Brand Navigation

15   16   17   18   19   20   21   7   6   5   4   3   2   1

In keeping with biblical principles of creation stewardship, Baker Publishing Group advocates the responsible use of our natural resources. As a member of the Green Press Initiative, our company uses recycled paper when possible. The text paper of this book is composed in part of post-consumer waste.

33614056425324

To my Lord and Savior, Jesus Christ.
Without You, this book would have never been possible.
Thank You for being a God of second chances.
This book is to Your glory and Your glory alone!

Contents

Contents

Acknowledgments

J am eternally grateful for all the people God placed in my life who have helped make this book possible.

First, I want to thank my husband, Dan, *the* most supportive husband in the world. I honestly wouldn't be where I am today if it weren't for you. Once upon a time, you believed in a young woman who didn't believe in herself. Since the day I met you, you encouraged me to chase my dreams. You have always believed I could do anything I set my mind to, including writing this book. Thank you for wiping away my tears through the hard times and cheering me on during the good. And thank you for your emotional, spiritual, and financial support, and for being so *incredibly* patient with me for the past twenty-six years. You are the love of my life! I couldn't imagine living in a world without you.

Next, I'd like to thank my son, Daniel, the light of my life. I know graduate school took time away from you, as did the writing of this book. Yet you never once complained—well, not much anyway. Thank you for giving me the freedom I needed to write this book by respecting my writing time every morning. Thank you for allowing me to use your life stories as examples and for helping me select which of my stories would best illustrate a point. And thank you for keeping it real and making me laugh with your wonderfully fun sense of humor. Your kind, gentle, creative, and carefree soul makes my heart dance!

I'd also like to thank the following people:

Dr. Craig Hazen, for encouraging me to write this book. It was your faith in me that gave me the courage and motivation to actually write the book contract that ultimately led to the publishing of this book through Bethany House. You not only persuaded me to write the book contract but also were with me when Andy McGuire initially contacted me about it. You and I read the email together. I'll never forget what you said to me: "Do you know what this means?" I didn't. All I knew was that I had a very important call to make, one that ultimately led to the publishing of this book. Thank you for all the editing you did on my book proposal, for reviewing my book contract, and for helping me successfully navigate the book publishing world. And thank you for believing in me, cheering me on, and telling me you were a fan. Your encouragement gave me the confidence I needed to proceed forward with this dream. I couldn't (and wouldn't) have done it without you.

Andy McGuire at Bethany House, for believing in me and giving me the incredible opportunity to write this book. What can I say? This book wouldn't exist without you. There are no words to express my gratitude. Thank you for selling my book to the publishing board so that the book in my head could become a reality in the world. Thank you for expressing my wishes to the Bethany team every step of the way. And thank you for your constant words of encouragement and all the other work you did that I don't even know about.

Helen Motter, my line editor, who became like an instant family member to me instead of a publisher during this process. Thank you for your kind words of encouragement and support about your opinion of the book's impact and value. Thank you for your edits, eye for detail, sound theology, and willingness to handle all the odds and ends needed to finish this book. This book would never have made it to the next phase in the publishing process if it weren't for you. I am so very grateful to Bethany House for giving me not only a seasoned editor but also a godly woman to work with. You will always have a special place in my heart as the wise and kind servant of Christ God gave me to edit my first book.

The publishing board, editorial staff, creative team, and sales and marketing team at Bethany House, for the hard work you all did to publish this book. You were the angels behind the scenes of this dream. You are the best. Thanks, everybody!

Andy, Helen, Helen's husband, Greg, and all the prayer warriors at Bethany House who prayed for me during the bewildering medical journey God put me on while I was trying to get the additional appendix and recommended reading resources Andy and Helen wanted to finish this book. How does a broken shoulder get misdiagnosed twice as a pathological fracture believed to be caused by an unidentified mass in my bone, first by the radiologist who read my MRI, and then by the radiologist who read my CT scan? If it wasn't for Dr. Wodajo (orthopedic oncologist who specializes in diagnosing bone tumors) who finally diagnosed my injury as a fractured tuberosity of my humerus bone, I still would be reeling in disbelief, thinking that an injury from a fall was in reality something more ominous. Your prayers, understanding, and compassion through this bizarre and terrifying life-altering experience, which I now believe was spiritual warfare, will never be forgotten.

My faithful readers: my mother-in-law, Betty Houser, and Beth Troutman and Rosalyn Han. Thank you all for the countless hours you spent reading, editing, and giving me feedback on my manuscript. Thank you for being honest with me and telling me what I needed to hear, not what I wanted to hear. And thank you for the constant words of encouragement, wisdom, guidance, and insight you gave me throughout the entire writing process. I truly couldn't have done it without you. And thank you, Beth, for giving me a book-signing pen years before I even got a book contract. You gave it to me because you knew it would happen, I wasn't so sure. Thanks for believing that I could do it.

Ashley Plitt, for all the hard work you did editing my manuscript and for clearing your schedule to meet my ever-changing deadlines. You make me look better than I am. I couldn't have done it without you.

All of my professors at Biola University, for being such godly men and showing me by example what it looks like to follow Christ. I also want to thank you for equipping me to write this book through the training you gave me in grad school. Thank you, Dr. Scott Smith, for being my thesis advisor and showing me that I had what it took to write a book. Thank you, Dr. Clay Jones, for showing me what it means to teach with passion for Christ, how to address the problem of evil and suffering, and how to write well in this field. Thank you, Professor Ken Samples, for arming me to defend the Bible; Professor Kevin Lewis, for teaching me sound doctrine and how to write efficiently (as only a lawyer could), and thank you for giving me permission to model my Belief Inventory Checklist off of your breakdowns of the major divisions of systematic theology in your document "Principio and Prolegomena"; Dr. John Mark Reynolds, for showing me how to interact with the culture; Dr. Gary Habermas, for equipping me to defend the resurrection; and Dr. J. P. Moreland, for showing me how to defend the Christian worldview in a world filled with unbiblical ones. You are all my heroes in the faith!

My church family at McLean Bible Church, for praying for me, encouraging me, and giving me opportunities that eventually led to writing this book. Thank you, Pastor Lon Solomon, for never straying from God's Word and for faithfully teaching its truths regardless of their popularity. And thank you for safely leading me through Israel, Egypt, Jordan, Greece, Italy, and Turkey, and teaching me about the archeological discoveries I talk about in this book. Thank you, Jane Daniel, for your godly example, encouraging words, and support over the years. Also many thanks to Cory Thurman, Jaclyn Hoffman, Nathan Reed, Chuck Sickles, Dan Callahan, Carol Denner, Isaac Fong, Chad Palmer, Eric Younts, and Guy Williams, for praying for me and encouraging me along the way. Your support has meant the world to me.

Lysa TerKeurst, for teaching me how to be authentic and real with my audience no matter what the cost, and for equipping me to effectively reach an exclusively female audience. I couldn't have done it without the training and guidance you gave me at "She Speaks."

Kathy McCabe, for allowing me access to your fun and creative brain as you helped me come up with titles for my chapters. And thank you for being willing to change your plans at a moment's notice and comb the streets of Washington, D.C., with me, documenting the evidence that God once mattered to our nation. I treasure your love of learning, adventurous spirit, and sense of humor. Thank you for your endless love, support, and encouragement along the way. I'm a better woman, wife, mother, Christian, and writer because of you.

My sister and brother, Catherine Reinke-Hompertz and Jeff Reinke, as well as Lindsay Yates, Kathryn Camp, Kelly Lee, Kasha Francis-Mitchell, Amy Normann, Leanne and Mark Rodgers, Jane Munson, Lynn Seitz, Jenny Park, Philip Alexander, and the gang at Solid Reasons, for all your love, support, and encouragement along the way.

Finally, I'd like to thank my mom, Elizabeth Evert, and my dad, Bill Reinke, for never giving up on me and always believing I'd do something of kingdom value one day. Mom, thank you for giving me my first NIV Bible, faithfully praying for me, and encouraging me along the way. Dad, thank you for giving me your deep love for God's extraordinary creation—the great outdoors—which taught me how to appreciate the simple things in life. And thank you both for passing your solid work ethic and morning genes to me, which enabled me to get up every morning at 4 a.m. to write this book. I love you both!

Introduction

God gave every Christian woman the ability to have extraordinary faith. Most want it, but confess they don't have it. Is there a secret to extraordinary faith? Yes! I believe there is. I believe the secret to extraordinary faith is fully engaging our minds, as well as our hearts, in our faith, because dynamic faith requires a healthy balance of both.

When Moses wrote to the children of Israel, who had wandered in the desert for forty years because of their lack of faith, he wanted to remind this new generation what God had done for their ancestors, so the children could enter the Promised Land and appropriate what was rightfully theirs. In doing so, he also challenged them to love God with their hearts, souls, and strength (Deut. 6:5). However, in the New Testament, when the religious leaders questioned Jesus about which of God's commandments was the greatest, Jesus quoted Moses' words in Deuteronomy 6:5, but made a change. Like Moses, Jesus told them to love God with their hearts and souls, but then He also told them to love God with their minds (Matt. 22:37). What does it mean to love God with our minds? It means that we know exactly what we believe about the following: the Bible, God the Father, Jesus Christ, the Holy Spirit, the resurrection, man, sin, salvation, angels, Satan, demons, the church, the end times, and eternal life. It also means that we know exactly *why* we believe what we do.

Let's face it. This is something we women are bad at. We're great at loving God with our hearts. Loving God with our hearts is easy, effortless, expected. And loving God with our hearts well is vital in order to have healthy faith. Where we fall short, however, is in clearly expressing what we believe and backing up those beliefs with solid reasons. We are easily able to say we believe in God, for instance, but are not as easily able to articulate the difference between the Christian view of God from other views of god in the culture, such as pantheism, panentheism, dualism, or henotheism. And when we state what we believe, more often than not, we give experiential reasons instead of rational ones for believing as we do. We believe God exists because we feel His presence when we are outdoors in nature. And we believe the Bible is true because we experience the peace and joy that comes from obeying its teachings.

While our experiential reasons are well founded, and may have led us quite far in our journey of faith, the question we have to ask ourselves is "Are these reasons enough?" Are the reasons enough to keep us securely grounded in our faith when it is challenged by hostile atheists? Are they enough for us to hold on to when the storms of life hit and doubts creep in? Are they enough to carry us through the times when life seems unfair, when anger, bitterness, and resentment take root in our hearts and we feel justified in giving up our faith or abandoning God? And are they enough for our unbelieving friends and family when we share Christ with them?

If we do not have more in our storehouse than experiential reasons for believing what we do, how do we respond to the Muslim woman in our book club who tells us that the reason she believes Allah is the true God of the universe is because she can feel his presence when she is outdoors? Or that the reason she believes the Qur'an is true is because she experiences the peace and joy that comes from faithfully obeying its teachings?

If we're honest with ourselves, I think most of us would admit that experiential reasons aren't enough. When we love God with our hearts in disproportion to our minds, our faith is out of kilter with the kind of faith God wants us to have. It is like a "wave of the sea, blown and tossed by the wind" (James 1:6). It is not able to survive our emotions that fluctuate from day to day. It is not able to endure hardships in life, like the loss of a parent or a terminal diagnosis for us or someone we love. It is not able to carry us through the darkest days when we are overwhelmed and feel like living life is just too hard. And it is not able to bear the pressures put on it by a culture hostile to Christianity. Good things become harmful when consumed in excess. Drinking water is essential for life, but if we guzzle too much at once, it chokes us. The same is true of our faith. Loving God with our hearts is essential for faith, but if we love God with our hearts at the expense of our minds, it harms our faith.

When we fully engage our minds in proportion to our hearts, however, our faith is balanced and in sync with the kind of faith God wants us to have. It is stable, and it allows us to always "be prepared to give an answer to everyone who asks [us] to give the reason for the hope that [we] have" (1 Peter 3:15). It is firmly grounded in God's objective truth on the days when our emotions run amuck and we are prone to believe Satan's lies instead of God's truth. It reminds us of the absolute certainty of Jesus' resurrection, so we remember that God's power that raised Jesus from the dead is the same power available to us today. It defends God's existence to us when we are in the midst of depression and it feels like He doesn't exist. And it equips us to stand up to the forces a relativistic, religiously pluralistic, Christless, and hostile culture puts on it. Good things thrive when properly balanced with other good things. If we drink enough water, eat well, exercise regularly, and get plenty of rest, our bodies will be healthy and strong. The same is true of our faith. If we love God with our minds in equal proportion to our hearts, our faith will be healthy and strong. It will be vibrant and dynamic. It will be resilient and enduring. It will no longer be ordinary. It will be extraordinary.

If you want extraordinary faith, this book is for you. All it requires is a willingness to do what it takes: lots of hard work, determination, and the courage to step outside your comfort zone and into a new normal—a normal in which fully engaging your head in your faith as well as your heart is as natural for you as breathing. Are you ready? I'm thrilled and honored to be taking this journey with you.

Soli Deo Gloria,
Patty

One

Yikes—"What is it?"

'll never forget the day it happened. I was heading upstairs, when I glanced out the window next to my front door and saw them. Four furry little heads stumbling around in my flower bed stopped me dead in my tracks. At first I was excited. I thought somebody's house cat had given birth to a litter of kittens underneath my house. This prospect delighted me. I'm a cat lover and proud owner of two Maine Coons, Jack and Felix. I'd like more, but my husband has made it clear that our house's cat limit is, and will always be, only two. I've abided by this strict rule for eighteen years. I'm an obedient woman. But what could he say if a momma cat decided to become a squatter on our property and make her kittens' new home our home? Surely he wouldn't make me toss these helpless creatures out into the wild with no place to go, would he?

With this thought in my mind, at the exact moment I was ready to go outside, one of the "kittens" looked at me. I froze in disbelief. It wasn't a kitten. I didn't know what it was, but it definitely wasn't a kitten. This beast had a square nose and big ears. It looked feral, uncontrollable, rabid. Was it a raccoon? A woodchuck? I had no idea. What I did know was that being unable to identify this pack of whatever *they* were, living underneath my house, made me afraid—afraid to go out my front door, afraid to walk in my yard, afraid to walk down the street to the mailbox to get my mail. What if their mother attacked me? I could see the headline: "Suburban Housewife Viciously Attacked While Getting Mail."

A few days later, I mustered the courage to get the mail. Before that, I had made my husband do it. But I was expecting a package. I didn't want to wait for him to get it for me. What can I say? I'm an impatient woman who has a hard time delaying gratification. So I shot up a few prayers asking for courage and protection and dashed off to the mailbox through my garage. On the way back, I saw a hefty red fox propped up on its elbows on my lawn staring at my front porch. Terrified, and with my heart pounding in my chest so loudly I could hear it beating in my ears, I sprinted back into the house, praying that my headline wasn't about to come true. Once inside, I darted to the window by my front door to see what the fox was looking at. Then I saw those four "unidentified" creatures jumping on each other's backs, playing. Then it hit me. The beasts living under my front porch were kits, not kittens, and the fox on my lawn was their mother, a vixen. When the mystery was solved, my fear went away. Now I had a different problem. Now I had to figure out how to get rid of them.

Fearing the Beast

Over the years, I've found that apologetics is for some Christian women what those unidentified baby beasts were for me. Something to fear. Some Christian women fear it because they don't know what it is. And they don't want other Christian women to know that they don't know what it is. Whenever women ask me in which field I got my master's degree or what I do for a living, and I tell them, I see in their eyes and hear in their responses *fear*. Their eyes expand like overfilled balloons about to pop as they smile at me and politely say, "How nice!" Then they walk away as though they weren't actually expecting an answer to their question. Their fear instantly ignites the flight response. These women can't get away from me fast enough.

Sometimes they hide their fear behind pride, and tell me they have no idea what apologetics is but are pretty sure they don't need it. Here, the fight response ignites. These women don't want to flee. They go at me like a bully on a playground, with fists flying. My question is "How do you know you don't need something if you don't know what it is?" One woman told me that since the apostle Paul didn't need it neither did she, whatever "it" was. She failed to see the irony in her statement.

Occasionally, women slump forward, look down at their feet, and avoid eye contact as they awkwardly tell me they have no idea what apologetics is, as if they are divulging their most shameful secret. Here, nothing ignites. Spiritual rigor mortis has set in. These women don't try to fight or flee. The mere mention of apologetics paralyzes them.

To you women who don't know what apologetics is or fear it, I say this: Not knowing what it is does not mean you should be ashamed of your not knowing. Nor is it something you should be afraid to tell other Christians about. Many Christians, both men and women, don't really know what it is. When I first encountered it, I had no idea. So if you are reading this, and don't know what apologetics is, don't feel bad. Know that you are not alone. What's important is what you're doing about it right now. You're reading this book. I'm excited for you. You are about to go on an adventure you will never want to end. Apologetics changed my faith and my life. I'm convinced it will do the same for you.

But maybe none of this describes you. Maybe you do know what apologetics is. Maybe you picked up this book because of its promise to transform your faith from ordinary to extraordinary. Maybe you've wanted to give your faith that special something that's been missing for a long time, and while moseying through a stack of Christian books at a bookstore or a women's conference, you came across this book and thought it might help. Transforming your faith is what you are interested in. You honestly didn't realize this book had anything to do with apologetics until just now! And you feel duped. And now that you know what it's about, you have no intention of reading any further because what you know about apologetics leaves a bad taste in your mouth.

Perhaps you feel this way because you see apologetics as a divider instead of a unifier and therefore want nothing to do with it. Perhaps you've seen it used to create a rift among Christian communities, families, and friends. Perhaps you've seen it used to intellectually tear individuals to shreds. Perhaps you've seen it used to shame, ridicule, and belittle unbelievers. If this describes you, please hear me out.

First, apologetics isn't inherently evil. That people have misused it in the past doesn't mean it's intrinsically bad. It's good. And shortly you will see that it is biblical as well. Second, please suspend judgment until after you've finished reading this entire book. You might see apologetics in a different light. And you might see that apologetics is the special ingredient that's been missing from your faith all along, the ingredient that has the power to transform your faith from ordinary to extraordinary. If you still don't see apologetics in a different light after reading this book, I'll respect your position. All I ask is that you wait until after you've read the entire book before making a final decision. Fair enough? So what is this beast we call *apologetics*?

Identifying the Beast

Simply put, *apologetics* is the rational defense for the truth claims of Christianity. Unlike other world religions, Christianity is true. Because it's true, its basic beliefs, such as God's existence, the reliability of the Bible, and Jesus' resurrection, for instance, can be defended much like a defendant can be defended in a court of law, with evidence and rational argumentation (a line of reasoning given to demonstrate the truth or falsehood of something).

Whenever I tell people I'm an apologist, I tell them I'm like one of God's lawyers here on earth. Like attorneys, Christian apologists use rational argumentation to defend the claims God makes in the Bible about himself and the world to those who don't believe they are true. Apologists help them to see that they are true.

The Bible teaches that God revealed himself to human beings in two ways: (1) through His created order, or the world, which theologians call *General Revelation* (Rom. 1:20), and (2) through God's Word, or the Bible, which theologians call *Special Revelation* (2 Tim. 3:16–17; 2 Peter 1:21). Through both, God tells human beings who He is, what He is like, and what His plan for the world is. While there is much we can learn about who God is and what He is like from General Revelation, there is much more we can learn through Special Revelation. For instance, through Special Revelation and only through Special Revelation, God tells us the following very specific facts about reality:

- That He exists and is the one and only God there is (Isa. 45:5–6)
- That there are two dimensions to this world: an invisible realm, which contains spiritual beings, such as God, angels, and demons, and a visible realm, which contains everything comprised of physical matter, such as the world and man (although there is a spiritual component to man as well, the soul) (Eph. 6:12; Luke 1:26)
- That it was He who created the world in which we live, and not the random forces and chance acts of evolution and natural selection (Gen. 1–2)
- That He created the world by speaking it into existence (Gen. 1:3–11)
- That He created man by forming him from the dust of the ground and breathing into his nostrils the breath of life (Gen. 2:7)
- That He and humans once enjoyed fellowship with each other in the garden of Eden until those humans disobeyed Him, fell into sin, and were cast out of the garden, losing that relationship with Him (Gen. 2:7–24; Gen. 3:1–24)

- How humans specifically fell into sin and that their sin affected not only the first generation, but all generations afterward (Gen. 2:15–24; 3:1–19; Rom. 5:12–21)
- The impact of a severed relationship with God for all of eternity, and our own spiritual and physical death as a consequence of our sin (Eph. 2:1–2; Rom. 5:12)
- God's plan of salvation to regenerate our dead spirits and restore our severed relationship with Him, through the atoning work Jesus did on the cross, for all who place their trust and faith in Him (Rom. 5:1–21; 10:9)
- That we are to live our lives under the lordship of Jesus and glorify God in all we think, say, and do (Gal. 5:19–20; 1 Cor. 6:19; 10:31; 2 Cor. 4:5)
- The reality of heaven for those who submit to the lordship of Jesus Christ, and the reality of hell for those who don't, as every human being's final and eternal destiny, a destiny that must be decided while still on earth (Luke 16:19–31)
- That this earth will pass away and a new heaven and earth will be established by God where believers in Christ will fellowship and reign with Him for all eternity (Isa. 65:17; Rev. 21:1; 2 Tim. 2:12)

Like it or not, this is the reality in which we all, not just some, live. You might say this is the "real world." The world in which we live is not some fantasy world created by Walt Disney. This is not "a kingdom far, far away" and we are not Sleeping Beauty or Snow White. Unlike God, we do not have the power to speak our own reality into existence like Brendan Fraser did in the movie *Inkheart*. Sure, it's fun to pretend we could, which is why movies like *Inkheart* are fun to watch. But that's all it is. Pretend! The reality in which we live is not generated by the ideas of imaginative people who create a reality we wish were true. Rather, reality is generated by God; it is true, and thus must be accepted by all who walk the earth.

This is where apologetics comes in. Because Christianity is true, there is a lot of historical, archeological, scientific, and philosophical evidence to support its beliefs. Apologetics is the art of taking all that evidence and organizing it in a coherent line of reasoning to demonstrate to ourselves and to others why it is more rational or reasonable to believe that Christianity's central beliefs are true than to disbelieve them.

Notice I did not use the word *prove.* I said the goal of apologetics is to take the evidence and organize it in a coherent way to demonstrate it is more *rational* or *reasonable* to believe Christianity's main beliefs are true than to disbelieve. Just as in a court of law, 100 percent certainty is not the goal. Rather, belief beyond a reasonable doubt is the goal.

Most things in life cannot be proven with 100 percent certainty. For instance, we cannot prove with 100 percent certainty that we will not die in a plane crash when we get on a plane. This is where faith comes in. Because we cannot prove it with 100 percent certainty, we need to take a leap of faith and trust that the pilots are well trained to handle the plane under any conditions. We must believe the statistical odds are with us that we probably won't crash.

The same is true with Christianity's central tenets. We cannot prove with 100 percent certainty that Christianity is true. What we can do is prove with as much certainty as possible, given the evidence God provides, that it is more rational to believe it is true than to believe it is not true. The rest must be taken by faith. This is where our hearts come in. Our minds can only take us so far. Strong faith is a dynamic interplay between our heads *and* our hearts. This is why Jesus told the Pharisees to include their minds in their faith in addition to their hearts (Matt. 22:37). This is why Peter also charged the church to do so, as you will see shortly.

The Beast Is Biblical

Apologetics is not something the modern church created. Rather it is something God created. When the apostle Peter wrote to the church, he told them to "always be prepared to give an answer to everyone who asks" them to give a reason for the hope that they have and to do it "with gentleness and respect" (1 Peter 3:15). What did Peter mean exactly? Let's unpack it to see.

Peter used the ancient Greek word *apologia,* which translated into English is *answer.* It means "to give an apology or defense, as in a court of law," and is where the word *apologetics* comes from. When lawyers defend someone in a court of law, they collect evidence to prove their client is innocent. They make strong defenses to represent their clients by preparing arguments (in a philosophic sense, not in an argumentative sense) that list reasons why their clients are not guilty. In addition, they prepare answers to tough questions they believe the prosecuting attorney will pose to their clients and witnesses to help them adequately prepare to testify on the stand. Lawyers prepare all parties involved beforehand *well,* so they are not caught off guard when it matters, when the prosecuting attorney pummels them in court.

What Peter is telling us, then, is that we need to know exactly what we believe about our faith *and* why we believe it, so when we are asked about our faith, we can articulate both responses. Peter is telling us to prepare beforehand *well,* so we will not be caught off guard when it matters, when people ask us about our faith. It looks like this: "I believe the Bible is the inspired, inerrant, and infallible Word of God for the following six reasons:"

1. There are approximately 25,000 manuscript fragments of the New Testament in existence today that reveal the Bible we now have matches 99.5 percent of the material the writers wrote in the original documents.

2. There are ancient writers outside the faith whose writings confirm the historical facts written in the Bible, such as Josephus, Tacitus, Suetonius, Pliny the Younger, and Lucian.

3. There are thousands of archeological discoveries that confirm the Bible's historical content.

4. Jesus' birth, life, ministry, death, and resurrection reveal that He fulfilled 332 Old Testament prophecies that pinpoint Him as the Jewish Messiah.

5. Fulfilling these prophecies is statistically impossible for any single human being to do.

6. The fulfillment of the biblical prophecies substantiates the Bible's supernatural origin.

Peter is also telling us that we should be able to answer tough questions about our faith. How well should we be able to answer thorny questions, especially those that are particularly prickly? We should apply the same standard. We should be able to answer them reasonably well. Notice the standard isn't perfection here. Jesus was the only One who could achieve perfection on earth. We are human. We are imperfect. Our goal is to do the best we can with the understanding we have at the time we are asked.

Don't worry if some of your answers don't come out as well as you would like. God can and will use anything, including our befuddled responses. And many times that's exactly what He does, so we know that He is the one who is doing the mighty work in people's hearts and not us. This doesn't take us off the hook, though. We are still called to do the best we can. It's important to understand, however, that apologetics can only do so much. Becoming good at answering tough questions well is achieved by taking risks, stepping out in faith, attempting to answer questions, messing up, and learning from our mistakes. Being good at our responses takes practice—lots and lots of practice.

Another thing Peter tells us to do is "always be prepared" (1 Peter 3:15). The word Peter used for *prepared* in the original Greek text implies the idea of being fit, as one would strive to become physically fit. For those of us who understand what getting, and staying, physically fit entails, we know it requires working out hard and consistently. Getting in shape and then quitting our workout regimen is not an option. Why? Because the moment we stop working out, our muscles begin to atrophy. Before we know it, we are out of shape and have to begin all over again.

There is no such thing as *maintaining* physical health. The moment we stop moving forward, we start sliding backward. Growth only occurs with change. And change requires motion. When we apply this to apologetics in our spiritual lives, it means we need to *continually* prepare ourselves to defend our faith without stopping, so we are *always* ready to give a response should somebody ask. And don't miss Peter's implication that someone will ask. But you already know that. Someone already has—many times. Right? The question we need to honestly answer is "How well did we do with our responses?"

If we stop the demanding, ongoing work necessary for giving a good defense for our faith, our defenses deteriorate just as our bodies do if we stop working out. This means that preparing to defend our faith is not a one-time thing. It is not enough to take one apologetics class, or attend one apologetics lecture, or read one book on apologetics, including this one. Immersing ourselves in apologetics is something we must constantly strive to do each and every day of our Christian lives.

For this reason, I believe apologetics is a spiritual discipline that should be incorporated into our quiet times alongside reading and studying our Bible, meditation, and prayer. Do you think that's a radical statement? I don't. Why? Because incorporating apologetics into our lives as Christian women is not a helpful suggestion; it is a biblical command (1 Peter 3:15).

Peter also tells us to defend our faith with "gentleness and respect." This is the most overlooked part of the verse; it is also the most important part. Sharing and defending our faith is an incredible privilege given to every Christian, not to be taken lightly. We should not think of it as something we *have* to do to fill some daily or monthly quota, so we can feel good about ourselves because we are fulfilling the Great Commission Jesus gave us in Matthew 28:19–20. Or so we sound good to others when they ask us how many people we've shared and defended our faith with recently. Instead, we should think of it as an amazing opportunity we've been given. Sharing and defending our faith flows from a heart full of love and gratitude, not obligation and duty.

It's important to remember that sharing and defending our faith is not about us. It's about the people whom God places in our lives. When we have the opportunity to do it, it is not about how good we sound. Instead, it is about helping people see that Christianity is true and that they have a need for Christ. It's about them, not us. We must never forget this.

It is also important to understand that when we use strong philosophical arguments, the goal is not to intellectually slam someone against a wall to knock them out so we can declare ourselves the winner. Rather it is to help them see where their thinking is illogical or where their current worldview is incoherent.

There is another important factor to understand. People become defensive when their beliefs are challenged, as they will be when we share and defend our faith. How defensive they become, however, depends upon the person. Some people become very defensive, while others only become somewhat defensive. How can we predict who will become defensive, and to what degree, and who will not? We can't. However, here's what I've found to be true. The level to which someone becomes defensive is directly proportionate to the level to which they feel something important to them is being threatened.

Whenever I share my faith with Mormons, for example, I know most will become very defensive. Why? Because I know when I'm asking them to consider the truth claims of Christianity in light of Mormonism, I am not asking them to simply switch from one belief system to another, with no repercussions. I am asking them to leave behind the familiarity and security they have known their entire lives. I am asking them to do something that might alienate them from their Mormon families and communities. I am asking them to do something frightening. And fear in most people, more often than not, manifests as anger (a response I anticipate and get).

When we speak with people outside the Christian faith, it is vital to remember that we are speaking to real people with real feelings who may be incredibly threatened by what we say. Therefore, we should be careful not to become impatient or irritated with them because they are not as easily swayed by our impressive arguments as we think they should be. Also, we must remind ourselves that the reason they are being defensive to the degree they are is because what we say is threatening their security. This is why Peter tells us to give our answers to others with "gentleness and respect." I cannot stress this enough. Sharing and defending our faith must come from a heart of compassion, empathy, and respect.

Finally, we must not overlook to whom Peter gave this charge. Peter gave it to the persecuted church in Jerusalem scattered throughout the provinces of Pontus, Galatia, Cappadocia, Asia, and Bithynia (1 Peter 1:1). He gave it to people who could—many of whom did—lose their lives for fulfilling this charge. Countless numbers were ripped to shreds by hungry lions. Many were burned at the stake. Others were crucified. Some were stoned to death. Several were beheaded. Peter knew Christians could die for what he was telling them to do. He told them to do it anyway.

Embracing the Beast

For those of you who didn't know what apologetics was before reading this chapter, do you still fear the beast? Now that you know what it is, are you ready to incorporate apologetics into your spiritual life as a daily spiritual discipline, as I've suggested? If your answer is *no* or *not yet* and the reason is because there is already too much on your schedule, imagine telling the first-century Christians to whom Peter initially gave this charge exactly what you think it will cost you. Your time? Your money? Your energy? Lunch with friends? An extra weekly Bible study? Less time in the gym? An evening out with your husband or significant other? A night at the movies? Your favorite TV show? A night out at the theater? I'll bet whatever you say would fall on deaf ears.

Discussion Questions

1. Before reading this chapter, did you know what apologetics was? If not, what did you think it meant?
2. Is apologetics something you fear? If so, why? What obstacles do you need to overcome to get past your fears?

3. Do you believe your faith reflects a healthy balance of engaging both your head and heart, or is your faith lopsided? If so, in what way is it lopsided? What do you think it needs to give it proper balance?

4. Incorporating apologetics into our lives on a daily basis as a spiritual discipline is essential for sharing and defending our faith. Do you agree? Why or why not?

5. How specifically can you begin incorporating apologetics into your life on a daily basis as a daily spiritual discipline?

6. Do you believe that learning how to engage your mind in your faith as well as your heart can transform your faith from ordinary to extraordinary? How do you think it might strengthen your faith? How do you think it might help you share your faith?

Part **1**

THE
ESSENTIALS

Two

You Are What You Believe

The decision to become an authentic follower of Jesus was the scariest decision of my life. What would my family and friends think? Would they look at me differently? Would they become uncomfortable around me? Would they view this proclamation as a prison sentence on my life? And what would my husband think? Would he think that I would no longer be the free-spirited girl he fell in love with? Or would he dread taking me to parties for fear that I might recite Scripture to his friends, or drop to my knees and pray for the people of Turkey? After all, isn't that what Jesus freaks do?

Prior to becoming a Christian, those were the perceptions I had of Christians. And now I was deciding to become one. Why? Surely, I thought, no one must know. I hoped it was possible to be a closet Christian and still follow Jesus authentically. But common sense, the Holy Spirit, and the Bible told me otherwise. As I sat in my favorite chair in my living room one nippy October evening, all my concerns, anxieties, and fears were swallowed up in the eye of the tornado that went swirling through my mind. All I could see was the path of its destruction and the damage it would cause. And after it lost momentum, what then? I could not see beyond the pile of debris consisting of the comfort and security I had known to be my life. Wouldn't it be easier to not make the decision? Certainly, except for one very important truth: After a ten-year journey through the world of Christian apologetics, I genuinely came to *believe* with all my heart, soul, mind, and strength that God indeed exists, Jesus really is God incarnate, Jesus really rose from the dead, and that Christianity is true. You see, God promises that if we seek Him with all of our heart, soul, mind, and strength, we will find Him (Jer. 29:13; Matt. 22:37; Luke 10:27). Well, I did. And continuing on with my life as it was before, living my life apart from God, was no longer an option. And I was terrified.

Beliefs. Everyone has them. Some are simple. Some are complex. Some are rational. Some are irrational. Some are true. Some are false. Some are sane. And some are downright crazy. Beliefs make Democrats, Democrats; Republicans, Republicans; Christians, Christians; and atheists, atheists. Wars are fought over them. Promises are kept because of them. Starving nations are fed in response to them. Beliefs have the power to divide and the capacity to unite. Nothing is as powerful as one's beliefs.

But do we know much about them? For instance, what *exactly* are beliefs? How are they formed? What makes some reasonable and others unreasonable? What is required to justify them? Are beliefs the same as knowledge? If so, how? If not, why not? And how do they affect our behavior? Must they have a connection to truth and reality? More important, what impact do beliefs have on our faith?

All people are aware that they have beliefs, with the exception of infants and very small children. However, many of us never take the time to think about our beliefs. We often don't see the connection our beliefs have on the choices we make, how those choices in turn influence our behavior, and how both beliefs and choices ultimately affect the lives we lead.

If we are to be women who love God with our hearts *and* our minds, we need to make examining our beliefs a priority. Because at a foundational level, Christians are people who *believe.* Think about it.

What term do people in the church repeatedly use to refer to other brothers and sisters in Christ? They call them *believers.* When I talk to Christian friends about a new acquaintance I've met at the gym or social gathering, the first question I get is "Is she a believer?" It's usually the only thing they want to know about the person. And whenever I reflect back on my life, and think about where I've been and where I'm going, I mentally divide my life into two time frames: the time before I was a believer and the time after I became a believer.

In the church, the word *Christian* is synonymous with the word *believer.* I wonder how many times this week you've used the two interchangeably. If you're like most Christians, I'll bet you've done it a lot. I know I have. For some of you, it may be too many times to count. The Bible does it as well. According to *The Strongest NIV Exhaustive Concordance,* the New Testament calls people who placed their trust in Christ *believers* twenty-seven times.[1] It calls them *Christians* three times: twice in the book of Acts (11:26; 26:28) and once in 1 Peter (4:16). Conversely, people who do not believe the same things Christians do are called *unbelievers.* The Bible calls them unbelievers as well—eight times.[2]

Why are Christians called believers? Because they get their very identity from what they believe, not from where they were born, the household in which they were raised, or the activities they do. For example, Christians are not called believers because they live in the United States, were raised in a Christian home, or attend a social gathering at their neighborhood church on Sunday mornings, or faithfully show up at church every Christmas and Easter. Again, Christians are called believers because of what they *believe.*

Christians hold a very specific set of beliefs about the Bible, God the Father, Jesus Christ, the Holy Spirit, salvation, man, sin, the world, its direction and history, and their place in it. And it is those beliefs, or set of Christian doctrines and dogmas, that make them uniquely Christian. At its very heart, Christianity is a belief system, not an activity. I love what the American pro-baseball-player-turned-evangelist Billy Sunday once said: "Going to church doesn't make a man a Christian any more than going to a garage makes him an automobile."[3] What makes a person a Christian is her Christian belief, particularly her belief in Jesus Christ as her Lord and Savior.

Because Christians are a people who believe, if we are Christians, it is vital that we know *what* we believe about our faith and *why* we believe it. We need to be very clear about *exactly* what we believe about God the Father, Jesus Christ the Son, the Holy Spirit, man, sin, salvation, the church, heaven, and hell. We also need to know all the reasons why we believe what we do. It's not enough to say we believe the Bible is God's Word or that it is true. We must know *why* we believe it is God's Word and why we believe it is true. When we know what we believe about our faith and why we believe it, the following wonderful things happen:

- We are able to confidently articulate what we believe and why we believe it to ourselves and others.
- We are able to *easily* share our faith with our unbelieving friends and family.
- We no longer fear sharing our faith because we definitely know what we believe and why we believe it.
- We get the extraordinary privilege of joining in God's work of redemption and assisting Him in bringing others to Christ.
- We are able to "demolish arguments and every pretension that sets itself up against the knowledge of God" and "take captive every thought to make it obedient to Christ" (2 Cor. 10:5).
- We strengthen our faith.
- We have balanced faith.
- We transform our faith from ordinary to extraordinary.

Knowing what we believe and why we believe it is not an option for the Christian, because as believers, our beliefs are at the very heart of who we are. Therefore, it is vital that we understand what beliefs are, how they are formed, the effect they have on our behavior, their relationship to truth, what makes them rational or irrational, how they differ from knowledge, and what is needed for them to be justified. First, what are they?

What Are Beliefs?

Beliefs are what we think about things and how we think things really are. They tell us what we think is true or false about ourselves, others, and the world in which we live. They reflect our personal opinions of things as well as our take on reality. They also reflect what is important to us and what is not. In short, beliefs make us who we are. There is nothing more important about us than our beliefs.[4]

How Are Beliefs Formed?

Our beliefs begin forming the moment we are placed in our mother's arms, the moment we start engaging in this magnificent and thrilling, yet unpredictable and frightening, world. From the moment we open our eyes and begin processing the stimuli in our world, we begin forming beliefs about things. For example, if every time a baby cries her mother responds quickly by feeding her or changing her diaper, the baby will form the belief that the world is a place where her needs are met. This belief will lead to another belief that the world is a safe place to live. Conversely, if every time a baby cries her mother fails to respond in a timely manner, or fails to respond at all, and doesn't feed her, and doesn't change her diaper so that a nasty rash sets in, the baby will form the belief that the world is a place where her needs are *not* met. This belief will in turn lead to another belief that the world is *not* a safe place to live.

These babies may not be able to articulate their beliefs because they don't yet have command of language due to a lack of development. Nonetheless, they will still hold these beliefs as a result of their experience with the world. And these beliefs will influence the choices each makes and how each lives her life. One will not be afraid to go out into the world and pursue her dreams. The other will be terrified to do so. That is, if she even dares to dream.

Our beliefs are not formed only by our experiences. They are also formed and influenced by significant role models, such as parents, siblings, relatives, pastors, teachers, and coaches, as well as friends and peers. Gender, language, socioeconomic status, culture, education, religion, and political affiliation also help us form beliefs. An educated Christian woman raised in a middle- or upper-middle-class urban home in the United States forms very different beliefs about herself, others, and the world in which she lives compared to an uneducated Muslim woman raised in a poor rural home in Kenya, for example.

Consciously and unconsciously, intentionally and involuntarily, willfully and unsuspectingly, our beliefs are the sum total of our lives. It's that simple.

Do Beliefs Affect Our Behavior?

If you really want to know what someone believes, watch what they do; don't listen to what they say. What they do will tell you what they really believe. Words are cheap. It's easy to say we believe exercise is a necessary ingredient for living a healthy life, yet most of us don't do it. Why not? Because we don't *really* believe it's important for being healthy. Of course, we don't say this. At least not out loud. It would make us look bad if we did. So we give all sorts of excuses for why we don't exercise. We don't have time. We can't afford to belong to a gym. We think walking on a treadmill is boring. But these "reasons" are nothing more than smokescreens to hide our true beliefs—that we don't *really* think we need to exercise because we still have normal blood pressure, cholesterol, and blood sugar levels, even though we haven't worked out. Deep down, we don't *really* believe we are at risk for a heart attack or stroke, so why bother exercising? We have more important things to do. And even if we do have high blood pressure, cholesterol, and blood sugar, we thank God for modern medicine, because all we need to do to keep our health in check is take a few pills. If we *really* believed we would have a heart attack if we didn't exercise, we would make the time, confess we know we don't have to belong to a gym to do it, and admit that other people think walking on the treadmill is boring too—the people who log hundreds of miles on the treadmill because they actually *do* believe their lives depend on it. Our behavior reflects what we believe. If we want to change our behavior, we have to change our beliefs.

Where Does Truth Fit In?

Beliefs should be based on truth. Without waiting for an answer, Pontius Pilate asked Jesus, "What is truth?" (John 18:38). Jesus claimed that He was the truth (John 14:6).

The word *truth* fills the Bible. It appears 224 times.[5] And those times only represent the word *truth*, not the derivatives of it. The phrase Jesus used in the New Testament as much as "It is written" is "I tell you the truth." He said it nineteen times in the book of Matthew alone. That Jesus said it is significant. It reveals that as the Son of God, Jesus not only claimed He *is* the truth, He also believed *in* truth. This implies Jesus believed truth could be known. Many in today's culture don't believe truth can be known. Some people assert there is no such thing as absolute truth. But by making such a statement, they are claiming the absolute truth that there is no such thing as absolute truth! They fail to see the irony. They neglect to see their statement as self-defeating because it asserts the very thing it denies.

The Bible is clear: Truth exists. It can be known. And when we ground our beliefs in it, we are rational. God gave us His Word so we could know truth. His truth. The whole truth. And nothing but the truth. Thus our beliefs must be grounded in truth. Jesus tells us that if we are truly His disciples and know the truth, the truth will set us free (John 8:32). Indeed it will.

What About False Beliefs?

When beliefs are not based upon truth and reality, they are false. The fact is, most of us hold some false beliefs from time to time. Sometimes we hold them because we hear things and accept them as true without bothering to take the time to verify whether or not they are true. Sometimes we hold false beliefs because even though we have given it time, we were somehow misinformed about an issue. Perhaps we didn't fully understand the topic and came to an erroneous conclusion. Perhaps we were given inaccurate data, which served as the basis for forming our beliefs. Sometimes we draw wrong conclusions from truthful facts. Sometimes our prejudices and biases get in the way. And every now and then, perhaps more than we'd like to admit, we see what we want to see even when the facts are not there. And sometimes, it's simply too emotionally painful to face the truth, so we distort or deny the truth so that reality is easier for our psyches to accept. Denial. Rationalization. Repression. Projection. Displacement. Regression. Psychologists call them *defense mechanisms* for a reason. We use them to help defend or shield ourselves from seeing the truth by distorting or denying reality. When we do, however, our beliefs are not in alignment with truth. All of us hold false beliefs for a myriad of reasons. That's not the issue. The issue is what we do with our beliefs when we discover some of them are based on falsehood.

What About Rationality?

When beliefs are based upon truth and reality, our beliefs are rational. However, when they are not, our beliefs are irrational. This distinction is important for us women to understand, because it is typically women who get the term *irrational* flung at them whenever they say things a bit too emotionally. Stating a truth in an emotional way does not make what we say irrational; our beliefs being severed from truth and reality do. So the next time your husband or co-worker or in-law accuses you of being irrational, demand some evidence that what you are saying is based on falsehood or that it is out of touch with reality. If either party cannot provide this because there is no evidence, then inform him or her that stating things in an emotional frenzy doesn't make you irrational. It just makes you emotional.

Whenever I need to discuss an issue with my husband that I am certain will make my emotions skyrocket, I email the issue to him instead of discussing it with him face-to-face. The reason I do this is because discussing the issue in writing keeps my emotions out of the equation. I find my husband and I are able to discuss delicate issues more successfully because what I say is being evaluated at face value instead of by my emotions. When my voice starts to elevate and quiver and my hands start flapping up and down like a bird taking flight because I think my husband is not hearing me, even *I* might accuse myself of being irrational, even though I know better.

Stating a belief emotionally isn't what makes a belief irrational. A belief being separated from truth and reality does.

Where Does Knowledge Fit In?

Beliefs result in knowledge. For beliefs to become knowledge, however, three things must be present.

One, we must hold a belief.

Two, the belief we hold must be true.

Three, the belief must be properly justified. In other words, there must be a good set of reasons for believing what we do. For example, I might believe my son is downstairs doing his history homework. If you asked me how I know for sure, I would tell you I saw him doing it when I went downstairs for something. Because I have good reasons for believing that my son is downstairs doing his homework, I have knowledge.

I do not have knowledge, however, if my beliefs are improperly justified. That is, when I lack good reasons for holding my beliefs. For example, I might believe my son is downstairs working on his history homework. And I might even be right. But if my reason for believing this is because he is not in the kitchen, my belief is improperly justified even though my belief is correct. Just because he is not in the kitchen does not mean he must be in the basement doing his homework. That he is not in the kitchen is not a good reason to believe he is in the basement doing his homework. It was a lucky guess. Maybe even an educated guess. But it was a guess nonetheless.

Beliefs can also lead to knowledge through experience. Have you ever read something, believed it was true, and thought you understood it? But then you experienced the very thing you read about, and the experience made you say, "Oh, now I get what the author was talking about." This is when a light bulb goes on, so to speak. Prior to your direct experience, you thought you knew what the author was saying. However, the experience made you realize you didn't really understand it when you first thought you did. Some people call this an "aha" moment. Others would call it an epiphany. This "aha" moment is when our beliefs turn to knowledge.

But here's the maddening thing about knowledge. We don't *know* that we don't know something until we know it. We may *think* we know something because we've encountered it many times. But we really don't know it at a gut level until we know it. Here's a general rule: If your *behavior doesn't change* when it should, if a change is indeed needed, and for the life of you, you can't figure out why you aren't changing your behavior because of the knowledge you think you have, it is almost always because you don't really know what you think you know. You may be able to state the belief you think you know (which is why you think you know it). However, there is no mental or experiential tie to your belief and words in the same way there is no mental or experiential tie to a parrot's. A parrot can say, "The phone is ringing" when it hears it ring, but the parrot doesn't know what it is saying, even though it sounds like it does. Children with autism do this with language as well. It's called *echolalia*. They are able to echo back what they hear. It sounds like they know what they are saying, but they don't.

There is nothing more powerful than gaining knowledge through our beliefs via personal experiences because when we turn belief into knowledge this way, we know what we know at the very core of our being, at a visceral level. And we are never the same again.

Our beliefs are ultimately about gaining knowledge. It should come as no surprise, then, that the Bible teaches God's people that attaining knowledge is what matters to God.

The word *knowledge*, or some derivative of it, appears in the Bible 1,250 times. That's over four times more than the term *belief* or some derivative of it appears. The word *knowledge* makes its first entrance in Genesis 2:9, when we learn about the Tree of Life and the Tree of Knowledge of Good and Evil. It appears again in Genesis 2:17, when God instructs Adam to refrain from eating the fruit from the Tree of Knowledge of Good and Evil. The word is then peppered throughout the rest of the Bible. In the Old Testament, the book of Proverbs alone has thirty-nine verses that talk about the importance of knowledge. Here are just a few:

- The fear of the Lord is the beginning of knowledge (Prov. 1:7).
- Then you will understand the fear of the Lord and find the knowledge of God (Prov. 2:5).
- For wisdom will enter your heart, and knowledge will be pleasant to your soul (Prov. 2:10).
- Choose my instruction instead of silver, knowledge rather than choice gold (Prov. 8:10).
- The wise store up knowledge (Prov. 10:14).
- Whoever loves discipline loves knowledge (Prov. 12:1).
- All who are prudent act with knowledge (Prov. 13:16).
- The discerning heart seeks knowledge (Prov. 15:14).
- Desire without knowledge is not good (Prov. 19:2).
- The eyes of the Lord keep watch over knowledge (Prov. 22:12).

Knowledge is spoken of in the New Testament as well. In the book of Matthew, Jesus' disciples came to Him and asked Him why He spoke in parables to the people, for He had just told the parable of the four soils to those who gathered by the lake. He said, "The *knowledge* of the secrets of the kingdom of heaven has been given to you, but not to them" (13:11).[6] In the book of Luke, when the religious leaders questioned Jesus about many things, including the rituals of hand-washing and cleaning dishes before a meal, Jesus said to them, "Woe to you experts in the law, because you have taken away the key to *knowledge*" (11:52).[7] When Zechariah was filled with the Holy Spirit and sang praises to God because his mouth was finally opened after having been struck mute for a time, he prophesied through the power of the Holy Spirit that his newborn son, John, was going to be a prophet of God who would prepare the way for the Messiah and would be the one who gives "his people the *knowledge* of salvation through the forgiveness of their sins" (Luke 1:67–77).[8]

Knowledge matters to God. Therefore, it should matter to us. I often hear Christians admonish other Christians by citing the apostle Paul's stern warning to the Christians in the church of Corinth "that knowledge puffs up" (1 Cor. 8:1). When they do, however, more often than not, what they mean is they think having too much knowledge is a bad thing. Why do I say this? Because their admonishment is almost always followed by the advice to stop relying on one's knowledge and instead start relying on one's feelings. There are two problems with this.

First, it is based on an inaccurate understanding of what knowledge is, as we just saw. Second, it isn't biblical. In the *entire* Bible, the word *feelings* and all of its derivatives are used only twenty-six times (*feel*, nineteen; *feeling*, two; *feelings*, two; and *feels*, three). And in each instance, the word is used only to describe an inner state of a person. The book of Proverbs doesn't say, "Wise men store up feelings," nor does it say, "Every prudent man acts out of his feelings." It is our *knowledge*, and not our feelings, that God emphasizes in His Word.

I'm not saying God doesn't care about our feelings. He does. It's just that God puts them in their proper place. Feelings describe an inner state. Happy. Sad. Mad. Glad. That's all they do. Feelings don't justify beliefs. Why? Because feelings are fleeting. Today I might feel something is true. However, tomorrow I might feel it's no longer true because my mood has changed. And feelings certainly don't replace knowledge.

Our problem as Christians isn't that we have too much knowledge. That isn't what people outside the church accuse us of. They don't go around saying, "Oh no, watch out for those Christians. They are really smart. They are able to articulate their beliefs so incredibly well and are able to defend their beliefs with such sound scientific and philosophical arguments that I am struck speechless because I don't know how to respond to them."

Rather, the opposite is true. We are more often called ignorant, uneducated, ill-informed, out of touch, childish, naïve, gullible, even stupid. I think we need to think twice when we use Paul's admonishment that knowledge puffs up. Paul didn't say it to be understood as a statement that Christians don't need knowledge. He said it so pride wouldn't get in our way, because he assumed we would have it. The truth is that Christians today aren't suffering because they have too much knowledge. We are suffering because we don't have enough. This is why God says in Hosea 4:6, "My people are destroyed from lack of knowledge."

Is It Important to Own Our Beliefs?

Because our beliefs are central to who we are, it is important that we take ownership of them. What does that mean? It means we take responsibility for what we think, even if it makes us unpopular. It means we use *I* statements when asked what we believe. It looks like this: *I* believe God exists. *I* believe Jesus Christ rose from the dead. *I* believe in objective truth. *I* believe the Bible is the inspired, infallible, and inerrant Word of God. When we own our beliefs, we have clear boundaries. We know what we believe and we know what others believe. There is no confusion. Our identity is strong to us and everyone else.

On the other hand, when we disown our beliefs, we lose touch with ourselves. We no longer know who we are or what we believe and neither does anyone else. When we don't take responsibility for our beliefs, we lose our sense of self and our sense of separateness from others. It is not clear where we end and another person begins. The lines are blurred. There is confusion. Our identity is weak. When we fail to own our beliefs, we lose ourselves. How do we disown our beliefs? The following are just a few ways:

- We disown our beliefs every time we don't say what we really believe in order to go along with the crowd.
- We disown our beliefs when we lead people to believe we agree with them when we really don't.
- We disown our beliefs when we say what sounds good or makes us look good instead of what we really believe.
- We disown our beliefs when we say what we think is expected of us.
- We disown our beliefs when we keep our mouths shut and stuff what we really believe deep inside.
- We disown our beliefs when we project our beliefs onto others instead of owning up to them ourselves.

Here's an example of the last way we disown our beliefs: Have you ever asked someone what they thought about something, only to hear that person skirt around the issue and tell you what other people think about it or what the church thinks? The scenario goes like this: Clare asks, "What do you think about sex education being taught in Christian schools?" Whitney responds by saying, "Some people think it shouldn't be taught." Did you notice what Whitney said, or didn't say? She didn't tell Clare what *she* thought about it. Instead, she told her what *other people* thought. This tactic leaves Clare guessing as to what Whitney thinks or believes about the issue. Maybe Whitney doesn't have an opinion, and if she does, she's not willing to take responsibility for it. Why do we disown our beliefs?

We usually disown our beliefs because of fear. What are we afraid of? Many things. We are afraid of being ridiculed. We are afraid of exposing our true selves to others. We are afraid of being labeled intolerant, bigoted, prejudiced, racist, or homophobic. We are afraid of appearing aggressive. We are afraid of seeming argumentative. We are afraid of being judged hostile. We are afraid of not being liked. We are afraid of being rejected.

Owning our beliefs takes courage. Lots of courage. And this is especially true for Christians living as we are in a culture hostile to Christianity. But we are fortunate. In America, Christians are only called derogatory names because of their beliefs. In other countries around the world, Christians are being slaughtered for their beliefs. But this should not stop us. Jesus told us we would be persecuted for our beliefs (John 15:20). And He called us blessed if we are (Matt. 5:10). If we are to be women who love God with our hearts *and* our minds, we need to own our beliefs—all of them. The good, the bad, and the ugly.

How Do I Begin Examining My Christian Beliefs?

Because knowing what we believe about our faith and why we believe it is so crucial for Christians, I've included a *Belief Inventory Checklist* at the end of this book to help you determine if you know what you believe and whether or not you are able to defend or justify those beliefs. The belief inventory doesn't list what you *should* believe specifically. As you most likely already know, Christians hold some beliefs that differ from others. What's important is that you know what *you* believe, and that you are able to defend and articulate *your* beliefs clearly. To help ensure that your inventory is thorough, I've listed the key doctrines of the Christian faith for you to examine. Doing the inventory is simple.

There are three columns. The first column is titled *I Know What I Believe,* the second is *I Can Defend This,* and the third is *I Own This Belief.* Carefully go through each subject one by one and determine whether or not you know what you believe about each and assess your ability to defend it. Also determine if you own the belief. If you know what you believe about a specific subject and can defend it well, put a check mark in the box for each column.

If you don't know what you believe about a subject, leave the box unchecked. Likewise, if you can't defend it (even though you may believe it), leave the box unchecked. Then assess whether or not you are owning the belief and mark the appropriate box. If you find that you don't know what a doctrine on the *Belief Inventory Checklist* means, that's a good indication that you probably don't know what you believe about that doctrine of faith. If you knew what you believed about it, you would know what it meant. Doing the inventory will allow you to identify your strengths and weaknesses. This will help you know where best to focus your time and energy as you engage your mind in your faith in addition to your heart.

When you do the inventory, make sure you are able to articulate your beliefs clearly, using your own words. Being able to state what we believe in our own words is the true test for whether or not we have fully understood and internalized our beliefs. When we can't verbalize a concept using words other than the ones we've read or have heard from someone else, it's typically because we don't fully understand the concept. When we truly understand something, we are able to easily explain it to others in our own words. If you can do this, give the item a check mark. However, if you have a hard time finding the right words, leave the subject unchecked for now. Most likely you don't understand it as well as you thought you did.

Once you've completed the inventory and identified your strengths and weaknesses, develop a plan that will enable you to strengthen your weaknesses. There are many ways to do this. Reading books and articles about the topic, attending Sunday school classes, and participating in online discussions are some good options. Choose whatever method works best for you. Here are some tips you can employ to ensure your success:

- Pray, asking God for His help in this endeavor. You can do all things through Christ who gives you strength (Phil. 4:13).
- Set achievable goals.
- Keep in mind that goals are attained little by little, one step at a time.

- Keep a positive attitude. The battle is ultimately won or lost in the mind.
- Eliminate the following phrases from your vocabulary: *I can't, If only, I don't think so, I don't have the time, Maybe not, I'm afraid, I don't believe I can.*[9]
- Replace them with the following: *I can, I will, I know, I will make the time, Absolutely, I'm confident, I'm sure.*[10]
- Choose one topic at a time. Doing everything all at once is too overwhelming.
- Don't be afraid to ask for help if you're having a difficult time grasping a concept.
- Once you think you've learned a concept, say it back to yourself out loud, using your own words.
- Make sure what you believe is biblical.
- If what you believe isn't biblical, take the bold move to change your belief so it aligns with God's truth.
- Once you've achieved a goal, express your gratitude to God.

My prayer is that you find the *Belief Inventory Checklist* useful. I also pray that, through it, your relationship with God will grow closer.

Your faith is directly proportional to your beliefs. My question to you is "What kind of faith do you want?" Ordinary or extraordinary? It all starts with what you believe. You *are* what you believe.

Discussion Questions

1. Have you ever thought about why Christians are called believers?
2. What are beliefs and how are they formed? Where do you think many of your beliefs were formed? How did you form them?
3. How have your beliefs affected your behavior?
4. Can you identify any false beliefs you may be holding? If you can, are you willing to change them? What about unbiblical

beliefs? Are you willing to change them so they align with God's Word?

5. Using your own words, why are beliefs rational or irrational?

6. How would you respond to a person who tells you there is no such thing as absolute truth?

7. With what should beliefs be justified? Why shouldn't our beliefs be justified by our feelings?

8. If our beliefs are properly justified, what will we have? If our beliefs are improperly justified, what will we lack?

9. Do you own your beliefs? If you don't, why do you think that is? What fears are preventing you from owning them?

10. When you do the *Belief Inventory Checklist*, how will you be able to identify your strengths and weaknesses? What plan can you implement to strengthen your weaknesses?

Three

Thinking Well Becomes Her

When my son was in middle school, I always asked him if he had any homework when I picked him up from school. It was my first question when he got in the car. Sometimes he said yes and sometimes he said no. It sounded reasonable enough when he said no, because sometimes he didn't have any homework. However, once when he told me he didn't have homework, I found out a few days later that he did poorly on a test. This didn't surprise me, because I knew he hadn't studied for the test. At least I saw no evidence that he had. Besides, he had told me he didn't have any homework, so I never followed up to make sure he did it. The first time this happened, I was patient and kind. I figured he'd study the next time. But then it happened again. The second time, I gave him a stern warning. The third time it happened, I was baffled. I gave him another firm warning and threatened to take away something he loved. I was certain it would work. It *always does*. But then it happened again.

I know Dr. James Dobson, *Focus on the Family*'s parenting expert, says parents should never yell at their kids for any reason, but I also know Dr. Dobson didn't have the challenge of raising my son. I always thought that if he did, he just might change his advice. One day, I snapped. I couldn't understand why this kept happening. Every time I asked my son if he had homework, he told me he didn't. Sure, I could have gone in and micromanaged his schoolwork, but then he would never learn how to do it himself. So instead, I did what every good mother does. I accused him of lying. He wasn't. He accused me of yelling. I was. And I was doing it against Dr. Dobson's fine advice! After ranting and raving and attempting to bring about a good result by lecture, my son finally said, "Mom, you asked me if I had homework. I didn't. I'm not lying." After I growled back, "What do you think studying for a test is called? It's homework!" he quickly shot back, "No, Mom, it's not."

Utterly dumbfounded, I asked him what in the world he thought it was. He told me he thought it was studying for a test. When I asked him what he thought homework was, he told me he thought homework was doing workbook sheets, writing papers, and doing reading and math assignments—all the other work that didn't involve studying for quizzes or tests. He then went on to tell me that they are different. I couldn't believe he was serious. But the expression on his face told me he was.

In that moment, I realized I'd broken the first rule for thinking well. I'd forgotten to clearly define my terms. Our definitions for homework were different. Mine was any type of schoolwork done at home, *including* studying for quizzes and tests. His was everything done at home *but* studying for quizzes and tests. He filed that into a different category of school life—the folder labeled "quizzes and tests," which was a different folder from the one labeled "homework." Today, I ask him *two* questions when he gets in the car: "Do you have any homework?" *and* "Do you have to study for any quizzes or tests?" The fighting has stopped. I am able to follow Dr. Dobson's advice after all.

If we are to be women who love God with our hearts *and* our minds, we have to learn how to think well. Women who think well are able to successfully fulfill the biblical command to "demolish arguments and every pretension that sets itself up against the knowledge of God" and to "take captive every thought to make it obedient to Christ" (2 Cor. 10:5). They are also able to "always be prepared to give an answer to everyone who asks [them] to give the reason for the hope that [they] have" (1 Peter 3:15). Women who know how to think well are also able to have better relationships with others because their communication with others is more clear, authentic, and real. They are also better equipped to share their faith with family and friends. How do we become women who think well? There are three simple steps we can take.

Step One: Clearly Define All Terms

The first step to thinking well is to clearly define all terms. Conversations can't be meaningful if the terms being used in the conversation have different meanings to the different parties involved.

To ensure we're not talking past people when we're having conversations with them, as my son and I were, it's vital to clearly define any terms in the conversation that could be problematic. This is especially important when having spiritual conversations. Doing so well, however, requires that we know a little bit about terms, words, and definitions and how problems can arise when we are not intentional about how and when to use them.

First, a term is "a concept with a precise meaning expressed by one or more words."[1] For instance, a *mother* (term) can also be called a *mom, mommy, mum, mummy, ma, mama,* or *momma* (words). Words can also represent different terms. For example, a *date* can be a fruit we eat or an evening out with a person in whom we have a romantic interest or even a casual friend. Terms and words are different. Terms are *concepts*. Words are *labels* we attach to concepts.

A definition, on the other hand, is a *statement* given to a term to give it meaning.[2] A woman who has a child is the definition of a mother. When I tell you I have a date, and include the information that I'm going out for the evening with my husband to dinner and a movie, my definition tells you to which concept of *date* I am referring—the evening out, not the fruit.

The following is what terms, words, and definitions look like when we put them all together: A *mother* (term) is *a woman who has a child* (definition) and can also be called a *mom, mommy, mum, mummy, ma, mama,* or *momma* (words). Seems simple enough, right? It's not. When we're not intentional about differentiating between terms, words, and definitions, we can get ourselves into all sorts of trouble in conversation. How? Well, we might talk past each other when we define terms differently, as my son and I did. Or we might not communicate our ideas clearly to others when we use vague or ambiguous terms. Or we might totally confuse the people we are speaking with because we've defined terms wrongly or have attached the wrong word to a term. Therefore, to avoid problems like these in conversations, we should be mindful to do the following things:

First, we should make sure we know the difference between terms, words, and definitions. Next, we should become intentional when speaking to others. This means we choose our words carefully by making sure we use terms correctly. It also means we only use terms we are able to define or explain well. Moreover, it means we make sure we attach correct words to them. This will clean up our side of the street. Then, we help the other person clean up her side of the street. How? We pay close attention to what she says and listen carefully for problematic words. When we hear one, we ask, "What do you mean?" inserting the problematic word into the question. It looks like this: "When you say you're spiritual, what do you mean?" Then we listen to how the person defines the term to see if it matches our definition. If it does, great. We know we are on the same page and won't be talking past each other. However, if our definitions don't match, we know we are coming to the issue from different places and will need to proceed accordingly.

The same idea holds true for ambiguous phrases. When someone says a phrase we don't understand, we should again ask, "What do you mean?" inserting the problematic phrase into the question. It looks like this: "When you say the Bible is full of contradictions, what do you mean by that?"

When using this technique, we will quickly discover that some people really don't understand some of the things they say, particularly when having conversations about spiritual things. It could be because they haven't spent much time thinking about spiritual issues, or it could be that they are repeating sound bites that are popular right now in our culture that sound good, make them sound smart, or are politically correct. The problem is, when they use sound bites, many times they don't know what they mean and can't tell us why they think they are true. To help us identify when people use sound bites, here are a few of the most common ones to look for floating around in our culture today about religion and Christianity:

- I'm not into institutionalized religion; I'm spiritual.
- I don't believe the Bible because it's full of errors.
- The Bible is full of contradictions.
- The Bible is sexist, oppressive, intolerant, homophobic, outdated, and irrelevant.
- The God of the Old Testament isn't the same God as the God of the New Testament.
- All paths lead to God.
- All religions teach the same thing.
- It's narrow-minded to say Jesus is the only way.

When we ask people what they mean when they repeat one of these sound bites, one or more of four things usually happens: (1) they become mute, because it has never occurred to them prior to that very moment to think about what the sound bite means. No one has ever called them on it before; (2) they might get angry because they don't know what it means and they project their anger onto us for asking them something they can't answer; (3) they might make something up on the spot. When people do this, they tend to talk in circles and make no sense. We may feel the urge to rescue them, but we shouldn't. We're doing them a favor. It usually motivates people to find out what the sound bite means. And (4) they will immediately return the question back to us and ask what we mean by the term or concept when we use it. This may be a tactic to get them off the hook, but we should recognize that we didn't use the sound bite. They did. We aren't the ones who should be defending what we believe. However, pointing this out will only aggravate the situation. Instead, if this happens, we should see it as an *opportunity* to share our faith. In fact, I love it when this happens, because it makes sharing my faith incredibly easy. Here's an example of what such a conversation could look like:

"Hi, Patty. What are you doing this weekend?"

"On Saturday, I'm going hiking with my family. On Sunday, I'm going to my church—McLean Bible Church."

"I've heard of it. Isn't it that really big church by Tyson's Corner?"

"Yes. Have you ever attended?"

"Me? No. I don't believe in institutionalized religion. I'm spiritual, though."

"Oh, when you say you're spiritual, what do you mean exactly?"

"Great question. First, tell me what you mean when you say you're spiritual."

"Well, when I say I'm spiritual, I mean I believe I'm made of a material body and an immaterial soul, which houses my intellect, will, and emotions. The immaterial aspect is what makes me a spiritual being, makes me *me*. Because I'm made in the image of God, who is also a spiritual being, I'm able to have a relationship with Him through prayer. I'm also able to have a connection with God, because the Bible assures me that the moment we declare with our mouth Jesus is Lord and believe in our heart that God raised Him from the dead [Rom. 10:9], God puts His Spirit into us [2 Cor. 1:22; 1 John 4:13; Rom. 5:5; Eph. 1:14]. Because the essence of who I am is spiritual, I'm confident that when my body dies, my soul will go to heaven, where I will live with God forever."

"Wow! Interesting!"

Notice I didn't shove my faith on her. She asked me to share what I meant by being spiritual, so I did. And I was able to work in the gospel at the same time.

Clearly defining terms helps us think well. It's the first step.

Step Two: Use and Evaluate Statements Properly

The second step to thinking well is to use and evaluate statements properly. Conversations (and spiritual conversations in particular) also can't be meaningful when we don't know how to properly use and evaluate statements that are made during our conversations with others. Therefore, to be successful at doing both, we have to know something about statements. Namely, we have to know what statements are, how we determine if they are true or false, what types of statements there are, and what their relationship is to one another. First, what are statements?

Statements

Statements are simply sentences that are either true or false. The sentence "Mary and Martha were sisters" is a true statement, while the sentence "Jesus spoke to His disciples in French" is a false statement. Both of these sentences qualify as statements because their truth values (true of false) can be determined. It's important for us to recognize that not all sentences are statements. For instance, commands are not statements. Commands tell us to do something. They don't require that we determine whether or not something is true or false. The command "Daniel, go to your room!" tells Daniel to do something—in this case, to go to his room. It would be totally inappropriate for him to respond by saying, "True or false." If he did, we would know he was not listening. Some types of questions are another example of sentences that are not statements. For example, the question "Who is Daniel Houser's mom?" requires my name for the answer, not a response of "True or false." Again, such a response would prove they were not paying attention.

There are two types of statements.

Self-Supporting Statements

The first type of statement is called a *self-supporting statement*. Self-supporting statements are statements that tell us whether or not the statement is true or false by the statement itself. Thus the name, self-supporting. The statement makes a report about itself. Self-reports, or statements people make about themselves with respect to their beliefs, dreams, goals, etc., are an example of self-supporting statements. It's important to note that self-reports can't be wrong. Self-reports are reports people make about themselves. If people say something is true about themselves, then we *must* accept it as true. Another example of a self-supporting statement is one that tells us whether or not it is true or false by the way it is constructed. For example, the statement "Jesus rose from the dead or He didn't rise from the dead" is true, and has to be true, because of how the statement is constructed. It covers all the possibilities by using the word *or*. Jesus either rose from the dead *or* He didn't. There are no other options. On the other hand, the statement "I read the entire Bible, and I did not read the entire Bible" has to be false because of the way the statement is constructed. I either read the entire Bible or I didn't. What can't be true is that I both read the entire Bible *and* I did not read the entire Bible simultaneously.

Supported Statements

The second type of statement is a *supported statement*. They are different from self-supported statements in that they require information or evidence from *outside* the statement to determine whether they are true or false. That's why they're called supported statements. There are several ways statements can be supported from the outside. The first is through a reality check. Does the statement match reality? For example, if someone made the statement "The church is full," and I want to verify that the statement is indeed true, I could simply go take a look inside the church to see how full it is. If the church is full, then the statement is true. If the church is not full, then the statement is false. Another way statements can be supported is by citing or consulting an expert. If I made the statement "The city that ranks number one for the most churchless residents in the United States is San Francisco," and I wanted people to believe my statement, then I would support this statement by citing research conducted by the George Barna Group (an expert in this field) to back up or support my statement. Yet another way statements can be supported from the outside is through deductive reasoning. In deductive reasoning, conclusions are drawn based upon other statements made that are assumed to be true. For example, if my son made the statement "Our cat, Jack, will not live to be fifty years old in human years," I could determine whether or not his statement was true by deducing that since no cat has ever lived to be fifty years old in human years, and since Jack is a cat, our cat will not live to be fifty years old in human years. Now that we know some basics about statements, let's look at how they relate to one another.

Relationships

Statements don't exist by themselves. Just like people, they are in relationship with one another. Therefore, it's important to understand what those relationships are and how they affect our ability to determine if statements we, or others, make are true or false.

One type of relationship that can exist between statements is one of independence. For a statement to be independent from another, it must not depend on the other statement for anything. It must be able to stand on its own. The statements "Jesus forgives people of their sins if they place their faith and trust in Him" and "My son, Daniel, went snowboarding last Saturday" are independent statements. The two statements have nothing to do with each other and therefore stand alone.

Another type of relationship that can exist is one of consistency. In logic, statements are said to be "consistent," when two or more statements are true and do not conflict with one another. For example, the statements "Mary was Jesus' mother" and "Mary gave birth to Jesus in Bethlehem" are statements that are consistent with each other because the two statements are true and do not conflict with each other. However, if I threw into the mix the statement "Mary gave birth to Jesus in Nazareth," then there would be an inconsistency between two of the three statements because one of them directly conflicts with another. The statements "Mary gave birth to Jesus in Bethlehem" and "Mary gave birth to Jesus in Nazareth" conflict because one of them is false. Mary could not have given birth to Jesus in both Bethlehem *and* Nazareth, because it is impossible to be physically born in two different places.

Another type of relationship that can exist is one of implication. In logic, this means that the truth value of one statement "implies" the truth value of another. The classic example of implication is the one our kids tend to care about the most during the winter. It is this: The statement "All schools in the area are closed if it snows" implies the statement "Some schools in the area are closed if it snows." Why? Because *some* is a subset of *all*. If it's true that *all* schools are closed if it snows, then it is also true that *some* schools are closed too. "All" schools can't be closed while "some" schools are not.

Another type of relationship that can exist is one of logical equivalence. In logic, in order for two statements to be logically equivalent, one statement must imply the second statement *and* the second statement must imply the first. The statements "No dogs are cats" and "No cats are dogs" is an example. If no dogs are cats, then it also has to be true that no cats are dogs. Now let's take a look at what all this has to do with our ability to think well.

Putting It All Together

As Christian women, one of our heart's desires is to share and defend our faith. For some of us, this also includes joining God in His redemptive work in bringing others to Christ. Being the relational creatures we are, most of us (if not all of us) also want to improve our relationships with others so that our relationships can be the very best they can be. In order to achieve these goals, it is vital we apply what we have just learned to the conversations we have with others. Here are a few tips to help you do just that:

- When making statements you want others to evaluate, make sure it is indeed a statement that can be evaluated. Also, when people make a statement to you that they want you to evaluate, again, verify that it is indeed a statement that can be evaluated. If not, politely tell the person why you are unable to evaluate the statement, and ask her to restate it.

- When people use phrases like "I believe, I feel, I wish, I desire, I want, or I need," recognize that they are about to give you a self-report. When they do, remember that self-reports can't be wrong. Self-reports are reports people make about themselves. If people say something is true about themselves, you *must* accept it as true. When you fail to recognize this and try to tell them that what they are saying is wrong, you breach this boundary and violate their very essence. A person's beliefs, feelings, wishes, desires, wants, and needs are what makes her *her* and not you. When you strip a person of what makes her unique, and remake her into your image, you take away a piece of her soul. Besides, claiming that you know another person's inner state better than she does is nothing short of sheer arrogance. The only one who is in a position to do that is God, and you are not God; so you must be careful not to pretend you are.

- When you give self-reports, you must be sure you are always honest. If you aren't, you will lead people to believe things about yourself that aren't true, which forces the other person to proceed forward in the conversation on faulty information. This is not fair. And God doesn't like it. Proverbs 12:22 tells us that "the LORD detests lying lips." Plus, false information about ourselves damages not only our relationship with God but also with others.

- When making a statement, you should be aware that sometimes it can contradict itself by the way you construct it. Therefore, it's important that the structure of your statement is sound, because healthy and fruitful exchanges can't take place if it is not. For the same reason, you should also listen carefully to the statements others make to be sure their statements are also logically sound. If they aren't, gently point out the contradiction and politely ask the person to restate them without the contradiction. If they won't, the best thing to do is tell them you don't understand what they are trying to say and drop the issue. Statements with internal contradictions make no sense, and it makes no sense to pretend they do.

- When making statements that require outside support, make sure you provide outside support, such as citing a qualified expert or utilizing your deductive reasoning skills. This is especially important when making statements about your faith. This is what it means to give an adequate defense. Besides, being able to do so will give you more credibility. Likewise, when others make statements that are not self-supporting, ask them politely to give you some outside support if you think it is necessary.

- If statements made need a reality check, make sure you give them one.

- When trying to persuade people of a specific Christian truth claim, the best way to do it is to follow in the footsteps of Sherlock Holmes and take people through a series of true statements until they draw the only logical conclusion that can be drawn. Deductive reasoning is a powerful skill. Use it! Sherlock did.

- If other people try to persuade you to draw certain conclusions from other statements they make, again follow Sherlock Holmes' lead and use your deductive reasoning skills to determine if the conclusion follows from the prior statements made. If it does, and there is no logical way around it, you must accept the conclusion as true even if you don't like it. However, if the conclusion doesn't follow from the prior statements made, you shouldn't accept the conclusion as true, no matter how much the person you are talking to wants you to. And sometimes, you may even want to accept the other person's conclusion as true because it's an emotionally comfortable conclusion. However, you must not. Thinking well requires that you don't forfeit your intellectual integrity. Ever!

- When making multiple statements, make sure the statements you make are consistent with one another. Likewise, when listening to multiple statements made by others, it's equally important that you evaluate all of the statements as a whole to make sure they are all consistent as well. If they aren't, respectfully point out which statements are inconsistent, say why they are inconsistent, and ask that one of the statements be withdrawn or modified to make them consistent. When you really start paying attention to the consistency of the statements other people make (and perhaps even your own), you might be surprised at how many statements are inconsistent.

- When making statements, if it is your intention for one statement to imply another, make sure it, in fact, does. However, if it isn't your intention, still be aware that sometimes the implication is made even though it wasn't your original intention. When this happens, people may or may not point it out. They typically only point it out if it causes what you say to be problematic. Similarly, when listening to multiple statements made by others, make sure one statement implies another if that is the speaker's intention. If it doesn't, point it out and ask the person to restate one of the statements.

- Be careful that you don't confuse the term *some* with the term *others* in statements. Doing so may change the meaning of your statements.

- If you intend to make logically equivalent statements, make sure the statements are, in fact, logically equivalent. This requires that both of the statements are true or false. The same is true when evaluating statements. Sometimes, when debating heated issues, the statement of one person will be logically equivalent to the statement of the other person.

However, neither person realizes it. Why? Because the same thing is being said in such a different way that it's hard to recognize that what's being said is logically equivalent. When this happens, the two parties involved usually go at it for a while until one party realizes it and says, "Oh, we're saying the same thing, but in different ways." She's right. In fact, it's the simple way of saying, "We're making logically equivalent statements." Sometimes, however, people will assert that two statements are logically equivalent when they aren't. When conversing with someone who does this, it's important to point out why the statements aren't logically equivalent. Perhaps one is true and one is false. Whatever the case, you should tactfully point it out so the conversation can move forward.

I hope you have found the above tips helpful. Of course, there are many more practical ways to apply what we've learned about statements to the real world. I am confident that having a good understanding of some of the basics about statements will give you the tools to do just that.

Understanding the ins and outs of statements enables us to think well. It's the second step.

Step Three: Don't Violate the Three Laws of Thought

The third step to thinking well involves not violating the three Laws of Thought or assumptions people hold as true so rational conversation can take place. In order for intelligible exchanges to occur, especially exchanges about spiritual things, basic rules must be employed to help guide our thinking and eliminate vague, contradictory, or ambiguous ideas. The three Laws of Thought are these basic rules.

Law of the Excluded Middle

The first is the Law of the Excluded Middle. This law says that a statement must be either true or false and therefore excludes the possibility of the truth falling somewhere in the middle. For instance, the statement "Jesus is the Son of God" is either true or false. Jesus is the Son of God or He isn't. There is no middle option.

Law of Identity

The second is the Law of Identity. This law says that if a statement is true, then it's true. The statement "Christianity might be true for you, but it's not true for me" defies this law. If Christianity is true, then it's true for me *and* it's true for you.

Law of Noncontradiction

The third is the Law of Noncontradiction. This law says that a statement cannot be true and false simultaneously. This means Jesus cannot be Lord and not Lord at the same time and in the same sense.

When having spiritual conversations, or any conversations for that matter, if the person with whom we are speaking neglects any of the three laws, we need to gently point out what law they are breaking as well as why adhering to the law is important. We also must make sure we don't violate any of the laws ourselves. Thinking well requires that everyone play by the same rules.

Einstein once said, "Thinking is hard work; that's why so few do it."[3] He was right. It is. And thinking *well* is even harder. If we want to be women who love God with our hearts *and* our minds, learning to think well is essential. Not only will it strengthen our faith and enable us to share and defend our faith more effectively, it will also improve our relationships. If I was a betting woman, I'd say that when we start thinking well consistently, our friends and family won't be able to stop saying, "Wow! Look at her. Thinking well becomes her."

Discussion Questions

1. Can you state a time when undefined terms or phrases caused problems as you were trying to discuss an issue with

someone? If so, what were they, and how did they affect the conversation? Could problems have been avoided if problematic terms or phrases were clarified early in the conversation?

2. How could the following terms or phrases become problematic in spiritual conversations: *God, spiritual, Christian, institutionalized religion, tolerant?*

3. When having spiritual conversations with people, have you ever heard the sound bites listed in this chapter? If so, what did you do? Have you heard other sound bites not on the list? If so, what are they?

4. Can you give more examples of sentences that aren't statements?

5. Can you think of a time when you told someone who was giving a self-report that what she was saying was wrong? Can you now see that such a response violates boundaries? How exactly did you do it? What was her response?

6. Discuss the relationship between providing outside support for statements and a person's credibility. Why else is it important to support your statement?

7. Discuss a time you've used deductive reasoning. Did your conclusions logically follow from your other statements? Discuss a time when another person used deductive reasoning. Did her conclusions follow her other statements? If they didn't, what did you do about it?

8. Did you ever consider that statements were in relationship with each other? Can you think of a time you violated any of those relationships? How about when others have violated them?

9. Can you come up with other statements you've heard in conversations that violate the three Laws of Thought? How did their violation impact the discussion?

10. Apply what you've learned about statements to the real world.

Four

A Bad Thought Day

*I*t happened the night we were stranded in Chicago. From the start of the trip, nothing had gone right. First, our plane was delayed. Next, we were given conflicting information about our flight. When we finally arrived in Chicago, the first leg of our trip, we found out we'd missed our flight to Washington, D.C. We also found out that the next available flight was the next *night*, not the next morning. This meant we were stuck in Chicago for nearly eighteen hours. Even though this wasn't our plan, I decided to make the best of it. I envisioned getting our luggage, taking a long, hot bath to wash away the day's frustrations, and spending a lazy morning having breakfast in bed while looking out the hotel room's picture window at Chicago's charming snow-covered landscape. Perhaps I could do a little day-after-Christmas shopping in the airport while sipping a peppermint mocha, and then finish off the evening with a deep-dish Chicago-style pizza for dinner. I even fantasized about going to Garrett's Popcorn and getting a tub of my favorite—CaramelCrisp—to take home with us. In that moment, I felt very grateful we were stranded at one of America's busiest, and largest, airports that had all the amenities I loved.

However, when we got to baggage claim to retrieve our bags, we found out they'd gone on to Washington, D.C. on a different flight and would not be joining us at our hotel. *What? Where am I supposed to put my contacts? How am I supposed to take off my makeup? How am I supposed to brush my teeth? What am I going to wear to bed? What am I supposed to do—sip a peppermint mocha while clawing my way around the hot, hectic Chicago airport shops blind as a bat with makeup smeared all over my face, wearing dirty clothes, looking like a street urchin? Are you kidding me?* These were the thoughts that *should* have been said in my *head.* Instead, I accidentally spat them out when I temporarily lost control of myself in the middle of baggage claim. After my outburst, my teenage son stood and stared at me, not quite sure what to do. But my husband did. We've been together for twenty-six years. He walked away and pretended not to know me. Why? Because he knew I was having a bad thought day—a very bad thought day—and he wanted no part of it. He was right: I was having a very bad thought day. And I wouldn't have wanted to be a part of it either.

When my thoughts unraveled before my husband, son, and the other curious onlookers in the middle of Chicago O'Hare International Airport the day after Christmas last year, I committed a fallacy called the *either/or fallacy* by presenting myself with a false dilemma. I erroneously believed I had only two options. The first option I thought I had was living out the blissful fantasy my mind fabricated at the gate. The second option I thought I had was having to spend the next eighteen hours in such dire straits that I wouldn't have been able to even splash some warm water on my face before going home, as though there were no water anywhere at the hotel or airport. In my mind, it was either the *best* of times or the *worst* of times. There were no *other* times for me.

The truth is there were several other options. For instance, I could've taken a shower at the hotel and used the soap provided so I wouldn't have to have makeup smeared all over my face. I could have bought new clothes at the airport and changed in the airport bathroom if my previous day's clothes were really that unbearably dirty. I could have bought new makeup at the airport as soon as the first store opened and fixed myself up before people began to pour in. I could have put my contacts in two glasses of water in our hotel room until we were able to buy more contact solution. I still could have shopped while sipping a peppermint mocha, eaten Chicago's famous deep-dish pizza for dinner, and gotten a tub of caramel corn at Garrett's Popcorn. It simply wasn't true that I had only two options. I couldn't see more options, however, because my thinking was flawed in my weary, stressed-out state.

When errors sneak into our thinking, we draw wrong conclusions and commit what are called *fallacies*. Fallacies come in different forms. Some fallacies divert attention away from issues being discussed and draw it toward irrelevant information. Others occur when information is ambiguous, vague, or unclear. Still others happen when there are problems with the logical structure of an argument. If we are to be women who love God with our hearts *and* our minds, we should know what the different types of fallacies are so we don't commit them. We also should be able to spot them creeping into spiritual conversations with other people so we can refute them. Why? Because avoiding a bad thought day on our part, and theirs, depends on it. The first type of fallacies to be aware of are called *Fallacies of Ambiguity*.

Fallacies of Ambiguity

Fallacies of Ambiguity occur when information is ambiguous, vague, or unclear. There are five Fallacies of Ambiguity we should be aware of.

Accent

The first Fallacy of Ambiguity is called *accent*. We commit this fallacy when we alter the meaning of a statement by adding emphasis to a certain word. For instance, if a friend of mine made the statement "We should not lie to our husbands," meaning that *wives* shouldn't lie to their husbands, and I repeated the statement back to her, but stressed the word *we,* so that it said, "*We* shouldn't lie to our husbands," I just committed this fallacy. Why? Because I changed her statement to mean that only *she and I* shouldn't lie to our husbands, implying that it's acceptable for other wives to lie to their husbands. When conversing with people God puts in our path, we must be careful not to change the meaning of their statements by accenting or emphasizing words they didn't intend to be accented. Likewise, we should make sure they don't emphasize any of our words, changing their intended meaning and therefore committing this fallacy.

Amphiboly

The second Fallacy of Ambiguity is called *amphiboly*. We commit this fallacy when our sentences are vague or unclear because of bad grammar. The following statement is an example: "For those of you who have husbands and don't know it, we are holding a free marriage conference this Saturday." This statement is supposed to mean that married women may or may not know that there is a free marriage conference being held this Saturday. However, what it actually says is that for the women who are married but don't know they are married, there is a free marriage conference being held this Saturday. As you can see, amphibolies can be quite funny! However, if we are to be women who love God with our hearts *and* our minds, we should watch how we grammatically construct our sentences so that we communicate our ideas clearly and precisely, unless our intention is to be funny. Similarly, when other people make statements that are poorly phrased, confusing their intended meaning, it's wise to rephrase their statement back to them and ask which of the statements reflects what they intended to say.

Composition

The third Fallacy of Ambiguity is called *composition.* When we commit this fallacy, we assume that what is true of the parts is also true of the whole. The statement "Each child must give a five-minute speech at the assembly, so the assembly will last five minutes" is an example. In this statement, it simply can't be true that the assembly will last only five minutes if each child gives a five-minute speech. If there are even two children giving speeches at the assembly, the assembly will last ten minutes. If there are ten children giving five-minutes speeches, the assembly will last fifty minutes. Therefore, when making a statement, we must be careful that we don't assume that what's true of the parts is also true of the whole. To avoid confusion, we should kindly point out to others why it is an error in thinking to do so.

Division

The fourth Fallacy of Ambiguity is called *division*. Division is the opposite of composition. We commit this fallacy when we assume that what is true of the whole is also true of the parts. The statement "Harvard University is a great school, so every student who attends must be a great student" is an example. While it's true that students who attend Harvard are typically more intelligent or gifted than the average student, there can be differences within the student body. For instance, some students are at the top of the class, some are in the middle of the class, and some are at the bottom of the class. To avoid this thinking error, we should make sure that we, and others, don't assume that what is true of the whole is also true of the parts.

Equivocation

The fifth Fallacy of Ambiguity is called *equivocation*. When we commit this fallacy, we change the definition of a term in the middle of an argument.[1] The argument "The only rational being is man. Women are not men. Therefore, they are irrational" is an example. In this argument, the meaning of the word *man* changed in the middle. In its first use, *man* was intended to mean *human beings*. However, in this argument, the meaning of *man* switched to mean "male," so that females were compared to *males* instead of *human beings*.[2] Changing the meaning of a term in the middle of an argument can dramatically change the direction of the argument. In conversation, be sure this does not happen, because doing so commits *equivocation*.

Now let's look at Fallacies of Distraction.

Fallacies of Distraction

Fallacies of Distraction divert attention away from issues being discussed and draw them toward irrelevant information. Logicians James Nance and Douglas Wilson call Fallacies of Distraction "street-fighting."[3] Why? Because Fallacies of Distraction are most often heard on the streets in everyday conversations. When they're used, people don't play fair. There are eight Fallacies of Distraction.

Ad baculum

The first Fallacy of Distraction is called *Ad baculum,* which is Latin for "appeal to the stick." We commit this fallacy when we attempt to move a person's position by using a threat. The following statement is an example: "If you don't give money to support AIDS research, you or your family will most likely get AIDS." People don't get AIDS because they don't give money to support AIDS research. People get AIDS when they receive blood transfusions of contaminated blood, share needles with people who are HIV positive or have AIDS, or engage in risky behavior that makes them highly likely to contract the HIV virus. Trying to get people to donate to AIDS research by scaring them into believing that they, or someone they love, will get AIDS if they don't is nothing more than an idle threat. Threatening others makes us bullies. Therefore, we should never do it. Likewise, when people verbally bully us in an attempt to get us to change our behavior or beliefs to match their expectations, we should not retaliate with idle threats, but civilly point out to them what they are doing and ask them to give us reasons why we should consider changing our position.

I have a few words of caution here. Most threats are idle. When they are, we should point out the threat. However, some threats are real. The Islamic Jihadists who kidnapped 219 Christian girls from Nigeria and threatened to kill them if they did not convert to Islam were making a real threat. Therefore, it wasn't a fallacy. It's only a fallacy when the person making the threat *can't* carry out the threat. In the example above about contributing to AIDS research, the person intimidating people on the phone into making monetary contributions can't carry out the threat. If we are threatened, our job is to assess whether the person can and *will* carry out the threat in order to know how to proceed forward in the conversation or action.

Ad hominem

The second Fallacy of Distraction is called *Ad hominem,* which is Latin for "to the man." We commit this fallacy when we verbally attack a person's character or personhood instead of her argument. The following statement is an example: "You believe God exists because you're crazy." Calling a person a name, such as *crazy,* has nothing to do with why the person believes God exists. The person may have all sorts of lucid reasons for believing in God's existence. For instance, she may believe God exists because there are several scientific and philosophical reasons for His existence, as well as many undeniable experiential reasons. However, because she was called *crazy,* she could derail the conversation by giving a mental health update to prove she is not crazy and so defend her honor. In doing so, the focus of the conversation changes to her mental health and character rather than about whether or not God exists.

In conversation, particularly political or spiritual conversations, it is vital that we don't attack people's character or personhood when we don't agree with their views. Calling people stupid, ignorant, immature, intolerant, homophobic, sexist, bigoted, racist, or prejudiced because they hold different views than we do are not legitimate refutations. They are spiteful tactics driven by emotion, not reason. Colossians 4:6 reminds us that our "conversation should be always full of grace, seasoned with salt." Calling people names or attacking their character, simply because we disagree with them, is far from gracious. Likewise, when others attack our character, we should kindly point it out and ask that they stay focused on the issue being discussed. Here's a tactful way to do it: "I'm not sure how your belief about my mental health is relevant to this discussion. If you'd like, perhaps we could discuss it later. However, for now, let's focus on the issue at hand. I'd really like to tell you the scientific and philosophic reasons for why I believe God exists, if you'll hear me out."

In my opinion, character defamation is one of the lowest forms of "street-fighting." Sadly, it's also the most frequently used against Christians *and* women in general. Because some Christians hold differing views from people in our culture about abortion, gay marriage, stem cell research, euthanasia, life support, and the age of the earth, their reasons for believing what they do are almost never heard out, considered, or even refuted. Instead, the individuals are called names or otherwise intimidated. The same holds true for women. When women state conflicting views, we are often labeled *childish, emotionally unbalanced, unstable, crazy,* or *insane.*

Ad ignorantiam

The third Fallacy of Distraction is called *Ad ignorantiam,* which is Latin for "to ignorance." We commit this fallacy when we assume something is true or false because it has not yet been proven otherwise. The statement "There is no proof that God exists; therefore, God doesn't exist" is an example. That a person can't empirically prove God exists with 100 percent certainty doesn't mean God doesn't exist. It just means that His existence hasn't been proven with 100 percent certainty. Likewise, when we assert God exists because His nonexistence hasn't been proven, we also commit this fallacy. Again, just because His nonexistence hasn't been proven with 100 percent certainty doesn't mean God exists. It just means His nonexistence hasn't been proven.

When asserting whether or not beliefs are true or false, we must make sure we don't claim they are true or false due to a lack of information to inform us otherwise and commit this error. When others make similar claims without adequate information, we should lovingly point out their error.

Ad populum

The fourth Fallacy of Distraction is called *Ad populum,* which is Latin for "to the masses." When we commit this fallacy, we make an unlawful appeal to the majority. The statement "Most people today don't believe the Bible is God's Word" is an example. Just because the majority of the population doesn't believe the Bible is God's Word doesn't mean the Bible isn't God's Word. It merely means that the majority of the population doesn't think it is. What the majority of people believe and what is actually true don't always coincide. Once upon a time the majority of the people in the world thought the earth was flat. We know now that it isn't.

When making statements, it's important we don't claim our statements are true simply because most people believe they are true. To do so is an error in thinking and commits *Ad populum.* When having conversations with others, if they commit this fallacy, we should politely point it out and ask them to give another reason for their belief.

Bulverism

The fifth Fallacy of Distraction is called *Bulverism.* C. S. Lewis coined the term after one of his fictional characters, Ezekiel Bulver, in an essay he wrote called "God in the Dock."[4] It is also called the *genetic fallacy.* When we commit this fallacy, we focus on *how* a person came to hold a position, instead of addressing the position itself. The statement "The only reason you believe in full submersion baptism is because you attended a nondenominational church that practiced it" is an example. When we commit this fallacy, we draw attention away from the issue being discussed—why people should be baptized by full submersion—and make the discussion about the church the person attended—a church that practiced it. Assuming that the only reason a person believes in full submersion is because the church she attended practiced it, however, is an error in thinking. Perhaps the reason the person believes in full submersion baptism is because of a lack of biblical support for the other forms of baptism, such as sprinkling or pouring.

The only time this statement wouldn't be a fallacy is if the person who made it sincerely believes it's true only because of the church she attended. The truth is, some people genuinely don't know what they believe or why they believe it, and they honestly do believe things only because of the type of home, or country, in which they were raised or because someone else told them what to believe, or their church did. However, we still should *never* assume people don't know why they believe what they do and accuse them of it. Rather, we should ask people to back up their statements with reasons. The truth, and not an error in our thinking, should drive how we proceed forward in a conversation. When people commit *Bulverism*, we should gently point it out and ask them to address the argument directly.

Chronological Snobbery

The sixth Fallacy of Distraction is called *Chronological Snobbery*. When we commit this fallacy, we state that the modern world is inherently superior to the ancient world or vice versa. For example, in his book *God Is Not Great*, the late Christopher Hitchens (who was a staunch atheist) committed Chronological Snobbery when he said,

> Religion comes from the period of human prehistory where nobody—not even the mighty Democritus, who concluded that all matter was made from atoms—had the smallest idea what was going on. . . . Today, the least educated of my children knows much more about the natural order than any of the founders of religion.[5]

In his statement, Hitchens asserts that religion is not true because religion was invented by people who were stupid. The reason he thinks they were stupid was simply because they lived in the past. In effect, Hitchens is claiming that time makes people smarter.

We commit this fallacy when we assert that things are either good or bad *solely* because of their age. It works both ways. For instance, some people will assert that all old things are good simply because they're old and that all new things are bad simply because they're new. On the other hand, others will assert that all new things are good simply because they're new and that all old things are bad simply because they're old. While the passage of time definitely has improved people's educational level and quality of life in much of the world, it nevertheless can't be used as the sole reason for believing something is true or false. The truth is some new beliefs and inventions are good while others are bad, and some old beliefs and inventions are good while others are bad. Each must be evaluated on its own merits to determine which are good and which are bad.

When making statements, we must make sure we don't commit this error by asserting beliefs are true or false simply because of the time frame in which they emerged. Likewise, when having conversations with others, we should see that they don't commit this error either.

Ipse dixit

The seventh Fallacy of Distraction is called *Ipse dixit,* which is Latin for "He has said it himself." We commit this fallacy when we cite an *unqualified* authority in support of an argument. The statement "There is no God; therefore, God doesn't exist," even if made by a very famous person, doesn't qualify the statement if the person is not a theologian qualified to argue for or against God's existence. While she may be an authority in another field, it in no way qualifies her to be an authority in the field of theology. Therefore, to cite a famous person's statement as proof that God doesn't exist is an error in thinking.

When making statements about what we believe and why we believe it, we must always take care to make sure we are citing *qualified* experts. Likewise, when people cite unqualified experts to support their arguments, we should kindly point out that while the person they cited may be an expert in a field, she is *not* an expert in the subject matter being discussed and to claim she is commits *Ipse dixit.*

Tu quoque

The eighth Fallacy of Distraction is called *Tu quoque,* which is Latin for "you too." This fallacy is committed when we dismiss arguments by pointing out discrepancies between people's arguments and their behavior. For example, when I tell my son to do his homework and he replies, "Why should I do my homework? When you were a child, you didn't do your homework," my son has committed *Tu quoque.* My son's pointing out that I didn't do my homework as a child is not a reason why he shouldn't do his.

When talking with people, we must be careful that we don't point out inconsistencies in their behavior as an excuse for dismissing their arguments and commit this error in thinking. And when other people commit it, we should respectfully ask them to only focus on and discuss our statement, not our behavior, unless the discussion is about our behavior.

Having said that, Christians are called to be salt and light (Matt. 5:13–14), which means our behavior *should* match our words. Throughout the Gospels, Jesus called the religious people of His day hypocrites for not practicing what they preached (Matt. 23:13). In his letter, James also reminds Christians to be doers of the Word and not only hearers of the Word (James 1:22). While it's true that bringing up our behavior in arguments to divert our attention away from the real issue being discussed is an error in thinking, it doesn't mean that our behavior doesn't matter. It does. God calls Christians to be holy because He is holy (1 Peter 1:16), and part of being holy involves living authentically so that our words and behavior match. Because the truth is when our words and actions don't match, unbelievers are the first to point it out.

Let's look at Fallacies of Form next.

Fallacies of Form

Fallacies of Form are problems with the logical structure of a statement or argument, which can lead people to draw wrong conclusions. There are five Fallacies of Form.

Apriorism

The first Fallacy of Form is called *apriorism*. We commit this fallacy when we make a hasty generalization. The following statement is an example: "Greg lied to me; all men are liars." In this statement, a generalization is being made that all men lie because one man lied. However, not all men are liars. Only this man, Greg, lied. Therefore, to accuse all men of the actions of one man is unfair. Each man should be judged by his own behavior. When conversing with others, we must take great care not to make swift generalizations about entire groups of people that are based on one person. And if we catch others doing this, we should point out not only why it's inaccurate but also why it's grossly unfair.

Circular Reasoning

The second Fallacy of Form is called *Circular Reasoning*. When we commit this fallacy, we assume the thing we are trying to prove. The statement "I know the Bible is true because the Bible says so" is an example. This is called circular reasoning because it reasons in a circle. This statement assumes the Bible is true, using that assumption as an argument for a reason why the Bible is true (because it says it's true). For the believer, this is not a problem because she believes God is the author of the Bible and therefore can safely assume it is true. However, this is not a credible argument to use with unbelievers. Therefore, when speaking with people, and especially unbelievers, we must be careful that we don't assume the very thing we are trying to prove and commit this error in thinking. We should also make sure others don't reason in a circle.

Complex Question

The third Fallacy of Form is called *Complex Question*. When we commit this fallacy, we ask a question in such a way that it excludes the possibility of giving a fair answer. It is also called *Loaded Question, Trick Question, Multiple Question*, and *Plurium Interrogationum,* which is Latin for "of many questions." The statement "Have you stopped nagging your husband?" is an example. If you answer yes, then you imply that you used to nag your husband. If you answer no, then you imply that you still nag your husband. The question is asked in a way that assumes you nag your husband and traps you into answering in a way that implicates yourself. For obvious reasons, asking loaded questions in conversations isn't playing fair and should be avoided by all parties. However, if a loaded question *is* asked in a conversation, it's wise to point it out and request that the question be posed in a different way.

Either/Or

The fourth Fallacy of Form is called *Either/Or,* also known as *Bifurcation, False Dichotomy, False Dilemma, Black-and-White Thinking*, and the *Fallacy of the Exhaustive Hypotheses.* As I stated in the introduction of this chapter, we commit this fallacy when we falsely assume that there are only two options from which to choose, as though there are no other options. The statement "If you don't get good grades in high school, you will have to work at McDonald's" is an example. It's important to note, however, that either/or fallacies are *not* committed when referring to the choice between absolute truth and falsity in which there truly are no other options. Instead, this fallacy is committed only when two (usually extreme) options or choices are presented as the only two options from which to choose, when in reality there are many.

Sometimes, we get stuck in Black-and-White Thinking and genuinely believe we have only two options, as I did when I was physically and mentally exhausted at the Chicago airport and was not thinking clearly. When this happens, we are fortunate if we have people who love us enough to help us see our error. Ecclesiastes says, "Two are better than one, because they have a good return for their labor: If either of them falls down, one can help the other up. But pity anyone who falls and has no one to help them up" (4:9–10).

However, at times we purposely make either/or statements to force others to believe there really are only two choices. Why do we do this? To force people into choosing the option we want them to choose. How is this done? By presenting them with the option we want them to choose, along with only one extreme alternative, making our option the only reasonable choice. When we do this, we aren't playing fair. And we aren't following Paul's charge to speak the truth in love (Eph. 4:15). Therefore, when we converse with friends, family, and acquaintances, we should make sure we don't manipulate them by presenting them with false dilemmas. Likewise, if they do this to us, we should lovingly point it out and openly articulate other possible alternatives.

Post hoc ergo propter hoc

The fifth Fallacy of Form is called *Post hoc ergo propter hoc,* which is Latin for "after this, therefore because of this." It is also called *False Cause* or the *Rooster Syndrome.* We commit this fallacy when we erroneously conclude that a sequence of time implies a cause-and-effect relationship. The statement "I'm not taking Daniel with me on picnics anymore because every time I do, it rains" is an example. While it might be true that it has rained every time Daniel has come on a picnic with me, it's simply not true that Daniel's presence caused it to rain. To suggest it does is to state an invalid cause-and-effect relationship. This is called the *Rooster Syndrome* because the rooster commits the same error in thinking when he falsely assumes that his crowing causes the sun to rise. To avoid making this error, we must make sure that we don't oversimplify our observations and state invalid causal relationships. And when others do it, we should point out why the causal relationships they are claiming are also unacceptable.

Women who love God with their hearts *and* minds know how to avoid making errors in thinking. They avoid errors by being aware of what they are and then examining the thoughts they are about to express to make sure they are error-free. This, of course, is easier said than done. Women who think well know that their goal isn't perfection; there is no such thing as a perfect human being. Instead, their goal is to simply do their best.

They themselves know how to spot errors. They spot them by simply asking, "*What* is this person trying to prove and *how* is she trying to prove it?" If they determine that the reasons given do not actually prove what the person is trying to prove, they know that most likely some error has been committed. Once they have determined that, they know their next task is to determine which type of error was committed. They then point it out. Women who think well know that conversations can't be productive or fair when errors in thinking are involved.

Abraham Lincoln said it best: "You may fool all the people some of the time; you can even fool some of the people all the time; but you can't fool all of the people all the time."[6] When errors in thinking creep into conversation—intentionally or unintentionally—people are fooled. To love God with our hearts *and* our minds, let's resolve to glorify God by not being women who fool others or who are easily fooled ourselves. Avoiding a bad thought day depends on it.

Discussion Questions

1. Have you ever had a bad thought day(s)? If so, was it because you committed an error in your thinking? If so, which one(s)? How could you have restructured your thought life to avoid the error(s)?

2. Discuss a time when someone else had a bad thought day. What happened? Did it derail the conversation? How so? What did you do about it?

3. Are there other examples of Fallacies of Ambiguity (Accent, Amphiboly, Composition, Division, and Equivocation)?

4. Can you give other examples of Fallacies of Distraction (*Ad baculum, Ad hominem, Ad ignorantiam, Ad populum,* Bulverism, Chronological Snobbery, *Ipse dixit,* and *Tu quoque*)?

5. Have you seen or heard other examples of Fallacies of Form (Apriorism, Circular Reasoning, Complex Question, Either/Or, and *Post hoc ergo propter hoc*)?

6. Discuss times when you have seen fallacies committed in TV media, newspapers, or advertising.

7. How do you think relationships would improve if errors in thinking were lessened and/or eliminated?

8. Do you think the quality of your life would improve if you avoided errors in thinking?

Part **2**

THE
AUTHORITY

Five

Heaven's Bestseller

You won't see it on the *New York Times* bestsellers list, even though it's the bestselling book on the planet. You won't find it on Barnes and Noble's must-read tables, even though it's the most widely distributed book on earth. And you won't know about its popularity, even though it outsells all the published books in the world. The Bible.

It isn't just a book. It is God's special revelation to the human race, and is heaven's bestseller. It's a story about who God is, what He's like, and what His plan is for the world through Jesus Christ. It's "alive and active" and "sharper than any double-edged sword" (Heb. 4:12). It's useful for "teaching, rebuking, correcting and training in righteousness" (2 Tim. 3:16). We women are masters at turning its text into beautiful rainbows, writing spiritual insights in its margins, and discussing its relevance to our lives with our closest friends. We know it has the power to change lives because we've seen it and experienced it. We read it, study it, and memorize it. But can we defend it?

That is, are we able to explain to an unbeliever, in one coherent sentence, what the theme of the Bible is? Do we know the basics of this book, such as the languages in which it was written, how it was divided, and what the relationship is between the Old and New Testaments? Can we explain how we know the Bible is the inspired and inerrant Word of God? Are we able to convince unbelievers that the Bible we have today accurately reflects what was written by the first-century authors? What about the canon? That is, how did the early church recognize which ancient documents were authorized and inspired by God? And what about the Apocrypha? What is it and where does it fit in? And why are there so many modern translations of the Bible?

If we are to be women who love God with our hearts *and* our minds, it's essential that we are able to answer these questions. Therefore, equipping ourselves to do so is the goal of the next three chapters. First things first: What is the Bible?

What Is the Bible?

The *Bible,* a term that comes from the Greek word *biblos,* is a collection of sixty-six books written by forty different authors in three different languages over a period of fifteen hundred years, and has a single theme: God's plan of salvation for the world through Jesus Christ. It is divided into the Old Testament and New Testaments. The word *testament* comes from the Hebrew word *berith,* which means "a contract or covenant between two people or groups." Therefore, each Testament expresses a covenant made between God and His people. The first covenant (Old Testament) is an arrangement between God and His chosen people, the Israelites, a people through whom His redeemer would come. The second covenant (New Testament) is an arrangement between God and the church Jesus established while on earth. The two covenants relate to each other in that the former foreshadows the coming of Jesus as the Jewish Messiah and Savior of the world, while the latter tells about the specific details of His coming: it depicts

Jesus' birth, life, ministry, death, resurrection, and establishment of His church.

Old Testament

The Old Testament was written in Hebrew and Aramaic (a common form of Hebrew), contains thirty-nine books, and has a Hebrew and Greek division. The Hebrew division divides the Old Testament into The Law (*Torah*), The Prophets (*Nevi'im*), and The Writings (*Kethuvim*). Each section contains the following books.

The Law: Genesis, Exodus, Leviticus, Numbers, Deuteronomy.

The Prophets: Former Prophets: Joshua, Judges, Samuel, Kings (in the Hebrew arrangement, the books of Samuel and Kings were one rather than two books each); Latter Prophets: Isaiah, Jeremiah, Ezekiel, The Twelve: Hosea, Joel, Amos, Obadiah, Jonah, Micah, Nahum, Habakkuk, Zephaniah, Haggai, Zechariah, and Malachi.

The Writings: Poetry: Psalms, Job, Proverbs; Five Rolls (*Megilloth,* which are the five sacred scrolls read during Jewish holidays). Ruth, Songs of Songs, Ecclesiastes, Lamentations, Esther; History: Daniel, Ezra-Nehemiah, Chronicles (again, the Hebrew arrangement places Ezra and Nehemiah together as one book and the two books of Chronicles also as one).

The Greek arrangement divides the Old Testament into the following five sections: The Law (*Pentateuch*), Historical Books, Poetry, Major Prophets, and Minor Prophets. Each of these sections contains the following books:

The Law: Genesis, Exodus, Leviticus, Numbers, Deuteronomy.

Historical Books: Joshua, Judges, Ruth, 1 Samuel, 2 Samuel, 1 Kings, 2 Kings, 1 Chronicles, 2 Chronicles, Ezra, Nehemiah, Esther, Daniel.

Poetry: Job, Psalms, Proverbs, Ecclesiastes, Song of Solomon.

Major Prophets: Isaiah, Jeremiah, Lamentations, Ezekiel, Daniel.

Minor Prophets: Hosea, Joel, Amos, Obadiah, Jonah, Micah, Nahum, Habakkuk, Zephaniah, Haggai, Zechariah, Malachi.

Why are there two divisions of the Old Testament? Because when the Old Testament was written in its original languages, Hebrew and

Aramaic, it was organized into the Hebrew arrangement. However, when the Hebrew Scriptures were translated into Greek in 250–150 BC in Alexandria, Egypt, the books were rearranged into the Greek format. The first Greek translation of the Hebrew Scriptures is called the *Septuagint* (LXX), which means "seventy" in Latin, named after the seventy Jewish scholars responsible for the translation.

New Testament

The New Testament was written in Koine Greek (which is a common form of Greek), contains twenty-seven books, and is divided into the following four sections: Gospels, History, Epistles, and Prophecy. Each section contains the following books:

Gospels: Matthew, Mark, Luke, John

History: Acts

Pauline Epistles: Romans, 1 Corinthians, 2 Corinthians, Galatians, Ephesians, Philippines, Colossians, 1 Thessalonians, 2 Thessalonians, 1 Timothy, 2 Timothy, Titus, Philemon

General Epistles: Hebrews, James, 1 Peter, 2 Peter, 1 John, 2 John, 3 John, Jude

Prophecy: Revelation

The Vulgate

Because the number of Christians who spoke Latin was growing, the *Septuagint* was translated into Latin by Jerome, was completed around AD 400, and is known as the Latin *Vulgate*. The *Vulgate* follows the Greek division. It's important to note that the *Vulgate* became the primary Bible for Christians for the next nearly one thousand years. For this reason, the first Bible translated into English, by John Wycliffe, completed around 1380, followed the Latin (and Greek) division.

Modern Bible

The Bible we have today follows the Greek and Latin divisions. However, today it is called the English division. There is one important thing to notice about it. It's topical, not chronological, which is different from the Hebrew division. However, within the topical division, the events are listed in chronological order for the most part. This can make understanding the biblical events in the order in which they occurred tricky.

If you want to gain a better understanding of the order in which the events of Christ occurred, I suggest reading Thomas and Gundry's *A Harmony of the Gospels*. In it, the authors harmonize the four gospels by arranging them in four parallel columns. They then list the events of Christ in chronological order within those columns so that the reader can clearly see which gospels recorded an event and which did not. It is an invaluable tool for studying the events of Christ in the order in which they occurred, where they occurred, and when.

How Was the Bible Written?

How the Bible was written is a hot debate between Christians and unbelievers. Christians believe the Bible is a supernatural book produced by God. Unbelievers say it's just another spiritual book written by mere men, like every other spiritual book on the planet. But if Christians are right, and the Bible is a special book that originated from God so that it's unlike every other spiritual book on earth, how did God write it? After all, didn't mere men, such as Moses, David, Solomon, Isaiah, Daniel, Jeremiah, Matthew, Mark, Luke, John, and Paul actually *write* the Bible? How the Bible was written is an issue of *inspiration*.

Inspiration

When we say the Bible is the inspired Word of God, we mean that God gave the Bible to human beings by inspiration. Inspiration in the biblical sense, however, is different from inspiration in the artistic sense. When we say the Bible was inspired, we do not mean that the men who wrote it were inspired to write it like Laura Hillenbrand was inspired to write the book *Unbroken* because of former Olympic track star Louis Zamperini's extraordinary ability to triumph over the unimaginable. Instead, we mean that through the ministry of the Holy Spirit, God *directed* the writers to write the Bible so that they wrote what God wanted them to write. How did God inspire these human authors? There are four theories.

The first is called *limited* or *partial inspiration theory*. This theory states that the *ideas* in the Bible, and not the actual words, are inspired by God. In this theory, God gave the writers the freedom to express His thoughts in their own way. However, because the writers were given this freedom, they made errors, especially when writing about historical, geographical, and scientific matters, even though the Holy Spirit guided them in their writing. Another version of this theory, called *confessional inspiration,* states something similar. It states that only the spiritual content of the Bible is inspired.

The second is called *mechanical dictation theory*. This theory states that God selected certain people to write down His words *exactly* as He dictated them to the writers, as if those doing the writing were human pens.

The third is called *neoorthodoxy theory*. This theory states that the Bible merely *contains* the Word of God. It states that the ancient writers wrote about their spiritual lives as best they could while they experienced God. However, because they were fallible human beings, some of what they wrote is wrong.

The fourth is called *plenary verbal inspiration theory*. This theory states that the whole Bible, not just parts of it, is inspired. This means that the Bible is inspired from the first word in Genesis to the last word in Revelation. Consequently, everything in it is inspired—everything—including its historical, geographical, and scientific content. That everything in it is inspired is called *plenary inspiration*, plenary meaning "full." In addition, this theory also states that the *words* in the Bible, and not just the ideas, are also inspired. That the words are inspired is called *verbal inspiration*. However, this part of the theory does not state that God dictated the exact words to the writers, as mechanical dictation theory asserts. Instead, it maintains that God guided the writers to express

His words to mankind through their own unique personalities and writing styles.

Of the four theories, which is the best? The plenary verbal inspiration theory has the most biblical support.

Biblical Support for Plenary Verbal Inspiration Theory

Throughout the Bible, the Bible claims itself to be the inspired Word of God. In the Old Testament, Moses and the prophets repeatedly stated that what they wrote did not originate from them, but rather were the *words* of God. For example, when they gave messages to Israel, they often first said, "This is what the LORD says," so that the Israelites would know that what they were about to tell them were *God's* words, not theirs. Sometimes they varied it and said, "The word of the LORD that came . . ."[1] They even introduced "the burden [oracle]" as God's *words* (Nah. 1:1–2; Hab. 1:1–2).

The writers of the New Testament did as well.[2] For instance, in Galatians 1:11–12, the apostle Paul *insisted* that the gospel he and the other disciples taught was not from human origin, but by revelation from Jesus Christ. In 1 Thessalonians 4:15, Paul said certain teachings were "according to the Lord's word." How could Paul make such a claim? Because Jesus commissioned the apostles to speak and teach authoritatively on His behalf through the ministry of the Holy Spirit—the Spirit of truth (John 14:16–17). For this reason, the apostles' words carried the same truth and authority as Jesus' words did (John 15:20). And because Jesus is God, the words they wrote (and preached) were God's words.

In addition, they also claimed that the Old Testament writings were the words of God, sometimes passed on to them by angels,[3] and the Holy Spirit in particular,[4] as well as other New Testament writings they didn't write.[5]

The two clearest passages that support plenary verbal inspiration are 2 Timothy 3:16 and 2 Peter 1:20–21. In 2 Timothy 3:16, the apostle Paul says, "All Scripture is God-breathed and is useful for teaching, rebuking, correcting and training in righteousness." There are a few things to notice here.

First, when Paul says Scripture is "God-breathed," he uses the Greek word *theopneustos*, which implies that the Bible comes directly from the breath of God, and not the work of man. Christian apologists Norman Geisler and William Nix point out that to omit "the divine element from the term implied by *theopneustos* as is done in rendering the phrase 'every inspired Scripture' or 'every Scripture inspired' in the America Standard Version (ASV) of 1901, and the New English Bible (NEB) of 1970," is an error.[6] Why? Because to do so is to lose the *full* meaning of the Greek word Paul carefully chose to communicate the truth to the recipient of this letter: Scripture originated from the Spirit of God, not man.

Next, notice that Paul says, "All Scripture is God-breathed," not just parts of Scripture. When Paul wrote this, he was writing to Timothy, who pastored the church at Ephesus. Because Paul believed his own death was drawing near, he was giving Timothy final instructions and encouragement before he died. If Paul had wanted to tell Timothy that only the content that dealt with spiritual issues was God-breathed, he would have said so. Instead, he was careful to point out to Timothy that "All Scripture is God-breathed" so that he could teach the Ephesians that every single word *and* idea in Scripture came from God and therefore "is useful for teaching, rebuking, correcting and training in righteousness." Now let's look at the second book of Peter.

In 2 Peter 1:20–21, Peter says that "no prophecy of Scripture came about by the prophet's own interpretation . . . *but prophets, though human, spoke from God as they were carried along by the Holy Spirit.*"[7] There are a few things to take note of here as well. First, when Peter wrote this, he, like Paul, knew he was going to die soon (1 Peter 1:13–14). He also knew there were false teachers in the church teaching false doctrine, just as there were false prophets in the days of old giving false prophecies (2 Peter 2:1). Some of the teachers were claiming Jesus couldn't be God. Others taught that He was God but not a man. Therefore, before he died, Peter wanted the Christians to whom he was writing to know that Jesus fulfilled the Old Testament messianic prophecies and therefore was the Jewish Messiah as well as both God and man, based on the facts that: (1) the prophets didn't invent the prophecies, or put their own interpretative twist on them, but wrote what they wrote because they were inspired by God, and (2) the apostles were sure of it because they witnessed Jesus fulfill these prophecies with their own eyes (2 Peter 1:16).

Next, Peter said the prophets "spoke from God as they were carried along by the Holy Spirit." Unlike Paul, who told us *what* was inspired by God (the very words of all of Scripture), Peter tells us *how* God produced the Scriptures. Namely, God inspired the prophets through His Spirit as He "carried them along"; in other words, God guided them by the Holy Spirit when they recorded their prophecies. But guidance doesn't imply possession, as the mechanical dictation theory asserts. Instead, it means that God wrote down His words through these men in a way that also allowed their backgrounds, personalities, and writing styles to shine through at the same time. As theologian Paul Little said in his classic book *Know What You Believe*, "This guidance would of necessity include their choice of words, since thoughts are composed of words, much as a theme of music consists of individual notes. Altering the notes alters the song."[8] I couldn't have said it better.

For these reasons, it's unbiblical to embrace the idea that (1) only parts of Scripture are inspired because God gave the biblical writers the freedom to express His thoughts in their own way, so much so that what they wrote was fraught with errors, even though the Holy Spirit guided them in their writings, as limited or partial inspiration theory proposes; (2) that God selected certain people to write down His words *exactly* as He dictated them to the writers, as if those doing the writing were human pens so that none of their personalities or writing styles seeped through as mechanical dictation theory affirms; and (3) threads of God's spiritual truth are contained somewhere in the Bible as the ancient writers wrote about their spiritual lives as best they could while they experienced God, but nonetheless made mistakes, as the neoorthodoxy theory advocates. Therefore, the theory with the most biblical support is the plenary verbal inspiration theory.

But just because there's biblical support to substantiate the claim that the Bible is the inspired Word of God doesn't mean that the Bible is inerrant (without error), does it? Actually, it does.

Inerrancy

Biblical inerrancy is an implication of biblical inspiration. Since *all* the Bible is the Word of God (2 Tim. 3:16; 2 Peter 1:20–21), and since God cannot err (Heb. 6:18; Titus 1:1–2), the Bible then must also be free of error. For this reason, Christians say, "The Bible is the *inspired* and *inerrant* Word of God." And this is precisely what Jesus taught.

Throughout Jesus' ministry, whenever the Pharisees or Sadducees challenged Him, He responded to them by saying, "It is written," and then stated a passage of Scripture as though it was absolute truth. And Jesus didn't just assert that parts of it were true. Jesus affirmed that even the sticky issues were true: from Jonah being stuck in the belly of a huge fish for three days (Matt. 12:40) to the resurrection (Matt. 22:30) and the reality of heaven and hell (Luke 16:19–31). Jesus also believed that God would bring about every event in history that He said He would in the Bible— absolutely everything. He said, "Until heaven and earth disappear, not the smallest letter, not the least stroke of a pen, will by any means disappear from the Law until everything is accomplished" (Matt. 5:18; Luke 16:17). And God inspired the apostle John to warn believers that if anyone added to His words, or took any of them away, He would deal with them accordingly (Rev. 22:18–19). When the full counsel of Scripture is examined, the Bible reveals that it is what it claims itself to be—the inspired (and therefore inerrant) Word of God.

Objections to Inerrancy

But how can we say the Bible is the inspired and inerrant Word of God when what's been taught from it in the past, and even in the present, is clearly wrong?

What people say the Bible teaches and what it actually teaches is not always the same thing. If my son reads *Hamlet* and tells me what he *thinks* the plot is, but is wrong, it doesn't mean Shakespeare made a mistake when he wrote it. It means that my son was mistaken in his interpretation of it. The truth is people have been perverting the Bible's teachings for centuries. Sometimes it's a genuine mistake made by well-intentioned people. Other times it's done on purpose to push a personal or political agenda. And sometimes it's done because parts of Scripture are difficult to understand. But that doesn't mean the Bible is full of errors. It just means that people trying to understand it have misinterpreted it.

But what about the Bible's teachings on how human beings came into existence and the age of the earth? Hasn't modern science *proven* that human beings are nothing more than a product of evolution, not a special creation of God, and that the age of the earth is in the billions of years, not thousands, making what the Bible teaches wrong and therefore errant?

It's important to realize that modern science hasn't *proven* anything. Evolution and the calculating of the age of the earth are *theories*, not undeniable facts. They are *theories* put forth by scientists who are doing their best to understand reality, just as theologians are doing their best to understand reality. Sometimes scientists are right and sometimes they aren't.

When my mother was pregnant with my older sister, her doctor told her to drink one beer every day because it would help her, and the baby, gain weight. Today, doctors say drinking alcohol is bad for a fetus. Which is it? Common sense tells us that drinking alcohol is probably bad for a fetus, but exactly how bad it is only God knows. The drug thalidomide comes to mind. This wonder drug, pushed by doctors in the '50s, was supposed to alleviate morning sickness, but the babies born to mothers who took it had severe deformities and often died prematurely. And what about mammograms? Scientists used to say mammograms saved lives because of early detection. Today, some scientists say they do more harm than good. Again, which is it?

The field of science changes its mind all the time. What scientists thought was right fifty years ago, or even ten years ago, they no longer think is right today. When the field of science asserts a theory, it's nothing more than that—a theory. The fact is sometimes what was initially thought to be right turns out to be wrong. And scientists know this. The problem is the average person on the street doesn't know this. Why? Because the media presents and promotes scientific theories as absolute, unalterable facts, when in reality they are only theories. Let's first look at the claim that evolution proves the Bible wrong.

Evolution is a *theory*, not a fact. While it's true there is lots of evidence to support the idea that *micro*evolution is true (changes made *within* species, such as Darwin's finches), there is no evidence to support the idea that *macro*evolution (one species changing into *another* species) is true.

Charles Darwin himself said that if the fossil record failed to show the transitional phases of one species turning into another species, then his theory is wrong. Guess what? The fossil record doesn't show it. In fact, it shows exactly the *opposite* in what is called the *Cambrian Explosion* (new species just appearing in the fossil record fully formed).

What's ironic is that the man who came up with this theory said that the one true test to determine whether or not his theory is correct would be in this transitional fossil record. If he's right, then scientists should be able to find millions, if not billions, of fossils of creatures halfway through their evolutionary process between animal types. Again, this hasn't happened.

The problem is our culture is *still* teaching Darwin's theory of evolution as *fact* despite the actual evidence, or should I say lack of evidence. And the media is keeping quiet when its so-called best evidence is found to be fraudulent, like Ernst Haeckel's embryos (one of the most egregious cases of fraud in academic history); Piltdown man (the skeleton that was supposedly from a primitive man, but actually was the skull of a human and the jawbone of an orangutan); the drawing of Nebraska man (which was inspired by one single pig tooth); Java man (which evolutionists claimed was a primitive man because a skullcap and single tooth of an ape was found next to the thigh bone of a human); and Neanderthal man (the so-called "missing link" based on fraudulent carbon dating of a skull, the second most egregious fraud case in academic history).[9]

What about Cro-Magnon man? Wasn't he authentic? And if so, isn't he the proof Darwin insisted upon?[10] Yes and no. In 1868, Cro-Magnon fossils were discovered in a cave, thought to be 23,000 to 27,000 years old, called Abri de Cro-Magnon, located outside a tiny village in southwestern France. As Jeff Miller points out in his article "Cro-Magnon Man: Nothing but a 'Modern' Man," evolutionists claim the fossils found in it are the "missing link." *ScienceDaily* said the Cro-Magnoids are the first beings who have an "anatomically modern" skeleton. Recent research also suggests that they are genetically the same as us. In fact, some say they are so similar to us in anatomical structure and genetics that many don't believe they are different enough to warrant their own category as primitive man. So what's the problem?

As Miller points out, the problem is, according to evolutionary theory, the skeletons must be in a transitional phase and *different* from us, not the same as us. In addition, their brains must be different from ours as well, because evolutionary theory asserts that the human brain is also a product of evolution. This means that early modern man *must* have been considerably less intelligent and skilled because their brains were not yet developed. The problem is there is no evidence of this either.

When we study ancient civilizations, we find the exact opposite. We find that humans have always had the intelligence and ability to perform amazing feats, ones we can hardly fathom. Without cranes, cement mixers/trucks, CAT scans, MRIs, ultrasounds, lasers, and airplanes, as Miller points out, early humans accomplished the following:[11]

- Built the Giza pyramids
- Built Stonehenge
- Built the immense temple of Artemis in Ephesus, Turkey
- Built a forty-foot statue of Zeus in Greece

- Embalmed people, preserving their bodies for thousands of years
- Conducted successful brain surgery
- Created a calendar from a study of the stars, with such precision that eclipses could be foretold and the cycles of the moon predicted with an error of only 33 seconds
- Constructed the Temple of the Sun from 140,000,000 adobe bricks they made
- Developed sophisticated irrigation systems and carved massive images into the ground, like birds, spiders, and whales, some of which covered 135 miles, images that can only be viewed from the air

Cro-Magnon man is not the new "missing link." What the Cro-Magnon fossils show is that human beings have always been modern man, just as the Cambrian Explosion suggests. The reason we'd like to think we're so much smarter than early man is because we're advancing forward today at exponential rates. Our progress, however, is not the result of the sophistication of our highly evolved brains. It's the product of the Industrial Revolution and modern technology. There is absolutely no evidence that our brains are more sophisticated than the brains of early man. In fact, our modern brains can't figure out how the ancient people did much of what they did, given the technology and resources they had. Sure, they were wrong about a lot of things. But so are we.

Some might argue that it was our highly evolved brains that started the Industrial Revolution and developed modern technology in the first place. Yes, but we did it on the backs of the advances made by early man. The field of mathematics was discovered by the early men of Mesopotamia, which laid the foundation for the field of science to emerge.

What about the primitive caveman drawings? Don't they suggest that early man was less intelligent and capable? No. The only thing cave drawings reveal is that human beings lived in caves and made their walls their canvases. While it's true that some of the drawings look like they were drawn by a primitive man, it's also true that others are fairly sophisticated and look like they were drawn by modern man. The truth is, some people have artistic ability and some people don't. If you were to ask me to draw a picture of a cow, the cow I would draw would look like it was drawn by a three-year-old. However, if you asked my dad to draw a cow, it would actually look like a cow. Not all humans have the same abilities. That some of the drawings look like they were drawn by a primitive man doesn't necessarily mean that they were drawn by a human with significantly less intelligence than ours. What it means is that they were drawn by a human who couldn't draw very well. Artistic ability is not a measure of intelligence, unless artistic intelligence is our only measure.

At the same time the media is pushing evolution as fact, it is also attacking alternative theories like creationism and intelligent design (irreducible complexity at the molecular level in the universe that lends support to the idea that the universe was designed by an intelligent agent) as viable substitutes. Why is this? Because our culture doesn't like the implications of other alternatives. If Darwin's theory of evolution is right, and human beings appeared on earth as a result of random, chance forces, then we can do whatever we want and are accountable to no one. However, if there is some intelligent agent, like God, who created us, it means we are not free to do whatever we want. It means we will one day be held accountable for our actions. Many in our culture don't like this.

Does this mean that evolution should *not* be taught in public schools? No. What it means is that when it is taught, it should be taught *truthfully*, for the *theory* it is, not presented as absolute fact. And the two types of evolution, micro and macro, should be differentiated. In addition, it should also be taught *alongside* creationism and intelligent design so that students can decide for themselves which explanation of reality they believe best fits the data. As it stands in America today, with the exception of the Bible Belt—which can err in the opposite direction—students are not given a choice. In some schools they are actually told they *must* believe Darwin's theory of evolution is true, because if they don't, they are told they will fail the course.

One of my friend's daughters took a class on comparative religion at a public university in southern Virginia four years ago. On the first day of class, her professor instructed the students to write their religious beliefs, if they had any, and turn them in. My friend's daughter did a smashing job of stating her Christian beliefs and defending them with well-thought-out, cogent arguments. When she got her paper back, she was shocked by her grade. She got an F. She quickly found out why. There was a note on her paper, handwritten by her professor. The note said that if she didn't change her Christian beliefs, she would flunk the course. How did she handle it? She continued to hold on to her Christian beliefs and did not cower to her professor's threat. Fortunately, her professor didn't give her an F. He gave her a D, which allowed her to graduate. But here's what she did do. On the last day of class, she wrote a note to her professor on her final exam. She told him that she really enjoyed the class and thanked him for strengthening her faith in Christ through his challenges in class. I'm pretty sure God looked down on her and said, "Well done, good and faithful servant!" (Matt. 25:21).

Just because our culture puts forth what it claims are scientific *facts* about the world in which we live, which are sometimes at odds with what the Bible teaches, doesn't mean that the Bible is full of errors. We mustn't forget this when speaking with people who insist that scientific *theories* are scientific *facts*. They aren't. With that in mind, let's look at the objection that the earth's age proves the Bible wrong.

While geologists and astronomers believe the universe is 13.7 billion years old, and the earth 4.56 billion years old, these so-called *facts* are based on radiometric dating (also called radioisotope dating) and the mathematical calculation of the "distance to galaxies and the speed of light."[12] Let's look at radiometric dating because it dates the age of the earth, which is the issue at hand.

Here's the problem: It's not always accurate. We know this because when tests are done on rocks of which the ages are known, the ages derived from the tests are wrong. A group of eight scientists who call themselves the RATE group (Radioisotopes and the Age of the Earth) took rock samples from lava rocks formed in 1986 from the Mount St. Helens 1980 eruption and dated them using Potassium-Argon dating, one of the tests commonly used by geologists. The tests showed that the lava rock was between 0.5 and 2.8 million years old. In reality, it was twenty-nine years old.

At Mount Ngauruhoe in New Zealand, eleven samples were taken that were formed from the 1949, 1954, and 1975 eruptions, and were sent to Geochron Laboratories in Cambridge, Massachusetts, a respected lab for dating. Geochron dated the rocks from 0.27 to 3.5 million years old.[13] In reality, they were only sixty, fifty-five, and thirty-four years old.

If radiometric dating yields dramatically wrong results on rocks in which the ages of the rocks are known, how can it be trusted on rocks where the ages are unknown? Can we really say with intellectual integrity that we know for certain that the age of the earth is 4.56 billion years old, when the tests used to determine it consistently yield results that are millions of years off and we know it?

It's simply not true that scientists know for certain that the earth is 4.56 billion years old, because the tests used to determine its age are problematic. But again, in America's public schools and universities, it's being taught as absolute, undeniable fact. As Christians, we need to understand that it is not an undeniable fact. It is an educated guess. One that scientists *think* is right, *hope* is right, but may not necessarily *be* right.

Second, it's important to realize that the Bible's teaching on the age of the earth isn't clear, despite the claims of some Christians. For this reason, Christians are divided on the issue. Some Christians refer to themselves as Old-Earth Creationists, while others refer to themselves as New-Earth Creationists. I love what one of my favorite Christian apologists, J. P. Moreland, says about the issue. He says that three days a week he's an Old-Earth Creationist and four days a week he's a New-Earth Creationist. Why? Because he believes there are really good arguments on both sides of this issue—biblical arguments made by highly educated people, some of whom hold multiple PhDs.

As Christians, it's important for us to know that this issue isn't as simple and clear-cut as people outside the faith (and even inside the faith) would have us believe. And it certainly isn't the one undeniable fact that proves the Bible wrong, as unbelievers would like us to think. If we believe that the Bible is God's inspired and inerrant Word, and have really good reasons for believing this, then perhaps the best position to take on this is one of humility. Maybe we should admit that we may never know the age of the earth. Maybe the earth is billions of years old because that's what some of the tests show and that's what it looks like. But if God is who He says He is, maybe He made it look that old when He created it. Or maybe He didn't. Maybe it's only thousands of years old like some Christians say. The truth is neither side really knows for *sure*. Wouldn't the world be a kinder place if both sides on this issue could be humble enough to admit this?

It turns out that the Bible isn't a book like any other spiritual book on the planet written by mere men. It's a special book. It's a supernatural book. It's God's book. It's heaven's bestseller!

Next, let's zoom in on the New Testament and investigate how we can know why the New Testament we have today accurately reflects what was written by the first-century authors.

Discussion Questions

1. How would you explain to an unbeliever, in one to sentence, what the theme of the Bible is?

2. Compare and contrast the Hebrew and Greek divisions of the Old Testament. How are they similar? How are they different?

3. How could knowing the English division of the Bible help you when reading and studying the Bible?

4. What is the relationship between the Old Testament and the New Testament?

5. Do you agree that the *plenary verbal inspiration theory* is the most biblically supported position? Why or why not?

6. How do the other theories of inspiration compromise God's character and nature?

7. Do you agree that biblical inerrancy is an implication of biblical inspiration? Why or why not?

8. We are given a few objections unbelievers might have with respect to biblical inerrancy. What other objections have you heard? How did you refute them? How would you refute them now?

9. Do you know of other students who were threatened by teachers or professors for openly stating their Christian beliefs in class? If so, what were the threats? How did the student handle it? If it was your child, how did you equip him or her to handle it? How would you do so now?

Six

The Real Deal

cholars agree that the New Testament was written between AD 40 and AD 100. The question is, how confident are we that the New Testament we have today is the same New Testament that was written over two thousand years ago? The best way I know how to answer this question is by using an acronym developed by Hank Hanegraaff, also known as The Bible Answer Man. The acronym is M.A.P.S. and stands for Manuscripts, Archeology, Prophecy, and Statistics.[1] I love it because it helps me defend the reliability of the New Testament in an organized way, not letting me forget any of the essential ingredients needed for defending it well.

Manuscripts

The first letter stands for *manuscripts*. When God inspired the authors of the New Testament to write His message to mankind, they weren't able to go to the store and buy paper, because it wasn't invented until the second century in China. Instead, they had to write on clay, stone, papyrus (split reeds that were pressed and glued into sheets and then tied together to form scrolls), vellum (animal skins from calves, antelope, sheep, goats, cows, or bulls), leather, and parchment, as well as various items such as metal, wood, precious stones, potsherds, and linen. Because these materials are biodegradable, the original biblical documents, called the *autographs,* no longer exist. What *do* exist are copies of the originals. Scholars of textual criticism call these copies the *extant manuscripts* (MSS), *extant* meaning "still existing" or "not destroyed or lost."[2]

Unlike today, where exact replicas of originals can be reproduced on high-tech copy machines at what seems like the speed of light, copies in the ancient world had to be made slowly, by hand. The question is "How well were these copies made?" To answer this question, we need to look at (1) the number of surviving New Testament manuscripts, (2) the time lapse between the autographs and the earliest extant copies, (3) the accuracy of the manuscripts, (4) the Christian manuscript support outside of the New Testament, and (5) the non-Christian manuscript support.

Let's first look at the number of surviving New Testament manuscripts.

Quantity of Manuscripts

The more manuscripts and/or manuscript fragments a literary work has, the more authentic scholars consider the work. How does the New Testament fare?

It fares extremely well. In total, there are 24,633 manuscript portions of the New Testament in existence today. There are 5,309 Greek manuscripts that contain all or part of the New Testament, over 10,000 manuscripts of the Latin Vulgate, and 9,300 manuscripts of earlier versions in languages other than Greek.[3]

In contrast, the most surviving manuscripts for any other work of antiquity are those of Homer's *Iliad,* which has only 643. Next in line is Tacitus' *Annals,* which has only twenty, followed by Caesar's *Gallic Wars,* which has only ten, and Plato's *Tetralogies,* which has only seven.[4]

When we compare the number of surviving manuscripts of the New Testament to other ancient books, we find that the New Testament has 23,990 *more* than the next runner-up.

Next, let's look at the length of time between the date of the original work and the date of the earliest copies.

Time Lapse Between Autograph and Earliest Copies

The smaller the gap between the date of the original work and the date of the earliest copies, the less likely textual errors and legend or myth are prone to creep in. How does the New Testament do when put through this test?

Again, it does exceedingly well. When we compare the dates of the original texts and the earliest surviving manuscripts, we find that the time lapse between the two dates is extremely narrow. For instance, the original gospel of John is dated somewhere between AD 60 and AD 90. The earliest surviving manuscript, the John Rylands manuscript, is dated between AD 117 and AD 138.[5] This makes the time lapse between the original gospel of John and the earliest surviving manuscript only about fifty years. In addition, the two most significant manuscripts of the New Testament, the Bodmer Papyri and the Chester Beatty Papyri, date back to AD 200 and AD 250 respectively, which makes the copies separated in time from the autographs by only 100 to 200 years.[6]

On the other hand, the gaps between these two dates for other works of antiquity are much wider. For example, the gap between Homer's original work of the *Iliad* and the first extant copy is 400 years. The time interval for Tacitus' *Annals,* Caesar's *Gallic Wars,* and Plato's *Tetralogies* is 1,000 years.[7] Yet unbelievers today consider these documents historically sound while refuting the reliability of the New Testament.

When we compare the length of time between the date of the original work and the date of the earliest surviving copies of the New Testament to other classical works, we see that it beats its next competitor by about 200 years.

Next, we want to look at the accuracy of the copies.

Accuracy of Copies

Did the scribes who made the copies make mistakes? While most textual critics agree that there are more than 200,000 variant readings in the surviving New Testament manuscripts, which sounds like a lot, it's important to understand how those variants are counted. According to Geisler and Nix, if one single word was misspelled in 3,000 different manuscripts, it's counted as 3,000 textual variants, not one.[8] Therefore, Geisler and Nix say, "Once this counting procedure is understood, and the mechanical (orthographic) variants have been eliminated, the remaining significant variants are surprisingly few in number."[9] How few?

The New Testament has 20,000 lines. Forty of them (or 400 words) are in question. This constitutes only one-half of one percent. This means that 99.5 percent of the material in the New Testament is accurate. And of the variant readings, one-eighth are stylistic differences, such as missing letters, misspelled words, or transposed words. This means that only one-sixteenth of one percent (about fifty) are meaningful variants. However, not one of these affects any essential Christian doctrine. Not one.[10]

In comparison, Homer's *Iliad* has 15,600 lines. Seven hundred sixty-four of them are in question. This means 5 percent of the work has variations, which is ten times *more* variations than the New Testament, even though it's only three-quarters of the length.[11]

When we compare the number of variants in the surviving manuscripts of the New Testament to other ancient literature, we discover that even though it's one-fourth longer than the next runner-up, it still has 724 fewer variants.

Next, we want to look at whether or not other historical Christian documents *outside* of the New Testament confirm or deny the reliability of the New Testament.

Christian Support

When examining the Christian support outside the New Testament, we want to look at the early patristic fathers' writings because they lived during the time of the early church, when the church was at its purest and most unblemished form—when it was closest to functioning like the Acts 2 church. They knew which New Testament documents circulated throughout the early church as authentic Holy Scripture and which ones didn't. Therefore, what they cited is significant.

When we examine their writings, we find that the early church fathers quoted the New Testament 36,289 times.[12] Here's the breakdown:

- Justin Martyr (330)
- Irenaeus (1,819)
- Clement of Alexandria (2,406)
- Origen (17,992)
- Tertullian (7,258)
- Hippolytus (1,378)
- Eusebius (5,176 times).

In fact, the early church fathers cited the New Testament so much that even if there were no surviving Greek manuscripts in existence today, the *entire* New Testament, with the exception of eleven verses, could be re-created from the scriptural citations of these early church fathers.[13]

It's clear by the sheer number of times the early church fathers cited the New Testament that they viewed it as God's sacred Word that was accurate, authentic, and reliable.

Finally, we want to look at whether or not other historical documents written by people *outside* the faith confirm or deny the reliability of the New Testament.

Non-Christian Support

If other works of antiquity corroborate the events in the New Testament, works written by people who had no ulterior motive to fabricate the events, then there is good reason to believe the New Testament is reliable. Were there any such works?

Yes. For instance, Tacitus, a Roman historian considered to be one of the most accurate ancient historians, recorded that Pontius Pilate ordered Jesus to be crucified (*Annals*). He even implicitly stated that there were people who truly believed Jesus rose from the dead. In addition, Suetonius, Emperor Hadrian's chief secretary, wrote about the Romans kicking the Jews out of Rome because of the continuous quarrels and conflicts they had about Jesus. Furthermore, Josephus, a Pharisee and ancient Jewish historian who worked under Roman authority, wrote that Jesus was a teacher, miracle worker, and charismatic man with a group of followers who followed Him while He was alive and continued to follow Him even after His death.

In addition, the following New Testament events were documented by people outside the faith:[14]

- John the Baptist was martyred.
- James, Jesus' brother, was martyred.
- Jesus was from Nazareth.
- Jesus lived a righteous life.
- Jesus was crucified under Pontius Pilate, during the reign of Tiberius Caesar, during Passover, and He was thought to be the Jewish King.
- There was an eclipse of the sun at the very moment Jesus died.
- Jesus' disciples truly believed that Jesus rose from the dead the third day after He died.
- Jesus performed miracles others called "sorcery."
- Jesus' followers quickly multiplied and were as far-reaching as Rome.
- Jesus' disciples refused to worship anyone else as God.
- Jesus' disciples lived moral lives.
- Jesus' disciples worshiped Jesus as God.

When we survey the texts written by some of the most significant ancient historians outside the Christian faith, some of whom were antagonistic toward Christianity, we find that the New Testament proves to be reliable.

Archeology

The second letter stands for *archeology* and addresses the question "Is there any archeological evidence that confirms that (1) the places in the New Testament existed, (2) the people were real, and (3) the events actually happened?"[15]

Yes. New Testament scholar Dr. Craig Blomberg says, "Within the last one hundred years archeology has repeatedly unearthed discoveries that have confirmed specific references in the gospels, particularly the gospel of John—ironically, the one that is supposedly suspect!"[16] Discoveries like what?

The following are some of the archeological discoveries that have been made over the past several hundred years that confirm the New Testament's reliability:

- In 1888, remnants of the Pool of Bethesda (John 5:1–15) were found near the Church of St. Anne in the northeastern quarter of the Old City in Jerusalem, in the area called *Bezetha*, or *New Lawn*.[17]
- In 1897, F. J. Bliss and A. C. Dickie unearthed a 75-foot court with a pool that is believed to be the Pool of Siloam (John 9:1–41).[18]
- In 1961, a stone with the inscription "Pontius Pilate Prefect of Judea" was discovered and dates to AD 16–37, revealing that Pontius Pilate was a real, historical person who lived during Jesus' time (Matt. 27:2; Mark 15:1–15; Luke 23:1–5; John 18:38).[19]
- In the '90s, the ossuary box (or bone box) of Caiaphas, the high priest Jesus was taken to after his arrest in Gethsemane, was found, revealing that Caiaphas was a real person who lived during Jesus' lifetime (Matt. 26:3).[20]
- Also found in the '90s was the ossuary box of James, Jesus' brother, revealing that he existed as well (Matt. 13:55; Mark 6:3).[21]
- In 1968, the remains of a male between the ages of twenty-four and twenty-eight years old who was crucified in the

middle of the first century was discovered, verifying that crucifixion was a means of execution during the first century (Matt. 27:45–56; Mark 15:33–41; Luke 23:44–49; John 19:28–37).[22]

- Two tombs have been discovered and thought to be the actual burial site of Jesus. One tomb is located in the Church of the Holy Sepulchre in the Christian Quarter of the Old City in Jerusalem. In 1883, the Garden Tomb was found 100 yards or so outside the Damascus Gate. While there is disagreement as to which site is the correct site, both sites reveal that there were tombs in Jesus' time similar in structure and location to the tomb described in the New Testament (Matt. 27:57–66; Mark 15:42–47; Luke 23:50–56; John 19:38–42).[23]

- In 1357, a linen shroud believed to be the actual burial shroud of Jesus was displayed. It is 14.25 feet long and depicts an image of a naked, bearded man with long hair, who had been crucified. It is called the *Shroud of Turin*. While there is some dispute over whether or not it actually is Jesus' burial shroud, it still reveals that people were wrapped in linen cloth in preparation for burial, just as John describes Jesus was in John 19:40.[24]

Furthermore, recent archeological discoveries have shown that Luke's books, Luke and Acts, are much more accurate than historians once thought. For decades, scholars outside the faith insisted that the New Testament was full of errors because they believed much of what Luke wrote was wrong. For instance, when Luke wrote in 2:2 that Jesus was born when Quirinius, the governor of Syria, was taking a census, historians insisted he made a mistake because Josephus said Quirinius was the governor of Syria in AD 6, not AD 7. However, archeologists unearthed a coin in Antioch with Quirinius' name on it, which places him as the proconsul of Syria and Cilicia from 11 BC until after Herod's death. It turns out that Quirinius was the governor twice, not just once, as historians first believed.[25] Luke was correct after all.

In addition, in 1910, a monument was found that proved that Iconium was a city in Phrygia, supporting Luke's claim in Acts 14:6

that it wasn't in Lycaonia, as historians once thought—historians who again accused Luke of being wrong, but they turned out to be the ones who were wrong.[26]

Sir William Ramsey, one of the world's greatest archeologists who ever lived, initially believed that the book of Acts was written sometime in the second century. In fact, he was so convinced of this that he set out to prove it by meticulously scrutinizing all of Luke's claims in the book of Acts. When he finished, Ramsey changed his mind. He said, "Luke is a historian of the first rank; not merely are his statements of fact trustworthy . . . this author should be placed along with the very greatest historians."[27]

As my pastor, Lon Solomon, says, "The more you dig out of the ground, the more the Bible proves to be right." Despite the attempts by archeologists outside the church to discredit the New Testament with the latest archeological discoveries they believe will topple the Christian faith, there has yet to be one that has disproven anything written in the New Testament—ever.

Prophecy

The third letter stands for *prophecy*.[28] The Old Testament was written over a one-thousand-year period and contains several hundred references to the coming of the Jewish Messiah.[29] These Old Testament messianic prophecies are important because they were meant to serve as signposts to help us correctly identify the Jewish Messiah and Savior of the world. They were also meant to help us see that when they were fulfilled at some point in history, we would know with certainty that the Bible could only have been written by God. There are 332 messianic prophecies in the Old Testament. Has anyone in history ever fulfilled them? Yes. One. His name is Jesus. He fulfilled them all.[30]

The following is a list of some of the most significant:

- Born of a virgin (Isa. 7:14; Matt. 1:18, 24–25; Luke 1:26–35)
- Born in Bethlehem (Mic. 5:2; Matt. 2:1, 4–8; John 7:42; Luke 2:4–7)

- Came through the tribe of Judah (Gen. 49:10; Micah 5:2; Luke 3:23, 33; Matt. 1:2; Heb. 7:14)
- From the family line of Jesse (Isa. 11:10; Luke 3:23, 32; Matt. 1:1–6)
- From the house of David (Jer. 23:5; 2 Sam. 7:12–17; Ps. 132:11; Luke 3:23, 31; Matt. 1:1, 9:27; 15:22; 20:30–31; 21:9,15; 22:41–46; Mark 10:47–48; Luke 18:38–39; Acts 13:22–23; Rev. 22:16).
- Will be called Immanuel (Isa. 7:14; Matt. 1:23; Luke 7:16 [in this verse interpreted as "God has come to help his people."])
- Will be preceded by a messenger (Isa. 40:3; Mal. 3:1; Matt. 3:11; 11:10; John 1:23; Luke 1:17)
- Will begin his public ministry in Galilee (Isa. 9:1; Matt. 4:12–13, 17)
- Will have a ministry of miracles (Isa. 35:5, 6; 32:3–4; Matt. 9:35; 9:32, 33; 11:4–6; Mark 7:33–35; John 5:5–9; 9:6–11; 11:43–44, 47)
- Will enter Jerusalem on a donkey (Zech. 9:9; Luke 19:35–37; Matt. 21:6–11)
- Will be betrayed for thirty pieces of silver (Zech. 11:12; Matt. 26:15; 27:3)
- Will be accused by false witnesses (Ps. 35:11; Matt. 26:59–60)
- Will be crucified (Isa. 53:5; Zech. 13:6; Matt. 27:26)
- Hands and feet will be pierced (Ps. 22:16)
- Will be mocked (Ps. 22:7–8; Matt. 27:31)
- Will be crucified with thieves (Isa. 53:12; Matt. 27:38; Mark 15:27–28)
- Will be rejected by his own people (Isa. 53:3; Ps. 69:8; 118:22; John 1:11; 7:5, 48; Matt. 21:42–43)
- Clothes will be divided and awarded to the one who wins the lot (Ps. 22:18; John 19:23–24)
- Bones will not be broken (Ps. 34:20; John 19:33)
- Side will be pierced (Zech. 12:10; John 19:34)

- Land will become dark at time of his death (Amos 8:9; Matt. 27:45)
- Buried in a rich man's tomb (Isa. 53:9; Matt. 27:57–60)[31]

People outside the faith are quick to say that this doesn't prove that the Bible is God's inspired and inerrant Word and that Jesus is the Jewish Messiah because (1) the disciples could have changed the Old Testament text to make it look like Jesus fulfilled the prophecies and then wrote about them in the New Testament, (2) Jesus orchestrated His life in such a way so as to make it look like He fulfilled them and then had His disciples write about it in the New Testament, and (3) if Jesus did somehow happen to fulfill them, it happened by mere chance. Are they right? Let's evaluate each argument.

First, did the disciples change the Old Testament text to make it look like Jesus fulfilled the prophecies? No. The entire Old Testament was written by 450 BC. The Dead Sea Scrolls, the remarkable archeological discovery of thousands of ancient biblical manuscripts (or fragments) found in March 1947 by a Bedouin boy in the caves of Qumran, contain one complete book of Isaiah and fragments of text from every other book in the Old Testament with the exception of Esther.[32] Scholars date them from 250 BC to AD 68.[33] The book of Isaiah, which contains many of the key messianic prophecies, was found in Cave 1 in its entirety, in such great condition that it can be easily read as if it were written yesterday. Scholars date it between 335–324 BC and 202–107 BC.[34] How does it read?

According to Dr. Gleason Archer, it "proved to be word-for-word identical with our standard Hebrew Bible in more than 95 percent of the text. The 5 percent of variation consisted chiefly of obvious slips of the pen and variations in spelling."[35] This means that the book of Isaiah we have today matches the manuscript written 107 years *before* Jesus and His disciples were born, and that's if we use the lower-bound date. If we use the upper-bound date, it means that these messianic prophecies were written 335 years *before* Jesus and His disciples were born. This means that there is *no way* the disciples could have changed the Old Testament text to make it look like Jesus fulfilled the prophecies.

Next, could Jesus have orchestrated His life in such a way so as to make it look like He fulfilled the prophecies and then had His disciples write about them in the New Testament? Not all of them. While it's true that Jesus could have orchestrated some of them, like arranging a rich man (Joseph of Arimathea) to promise to bury Jesus in his tomb after He was crucified, or purposely beginning His public ministry in Galilee, or deliberately riding into Jerusalem on a donkey, there is no possible way He could have orchestrated others, such as His conception, so that He would come from the family line of Jesse from the house of David or be born of a virgin. He also had no control over what Mary and Joseph would name Him on the day of His birth. He also had no control over whom would be crucified next to Him—the two thieves. Therefore, while it's true Jesus could have orchestrated some of the Old Testament prophecies to make it look like He fulfilled them, there is no possible way He could have fulfilled others.

Finally, if Jesus did happen to fulfill all of the Old Testament prophecies, did He fulfill them by mere chance? The fourth, and last, letter of the acronym will help us answer this question.

Statistics

The fourth letter stands for *statistics* and looks at the statistical probability of one person fulfilling as many Old Testament messianic prophecies as Jesus did during one lifetime.[36] Are the odds in anyone's favor? Not even close.[37]

In *Science Speaks*, mathematician Peter Stone discusses the statistical unlikelihood of such a coincidence happening. He says that the possibility of even fulfilling just eight prophecies all in one lifetime is 1×10^{17} or 1 in 100,000,000,000,000,000. To wrap our minds around such a probability, Stone says imagine laying silver dollars two feet deep on the state of Texas. Next, imagine marking just one of those silver dollars and mixing them all together so no one knows where it is. Now imagine blindfolding yourself and trying to pick the marked silver dollar. What are the chances you would pick the right one? Exactly. Close to zero. And this is if Jesus fulfilled only *eight* prophecies.[38]

Stone also calculated the probability of Jesus' fulfilling forty-eight prophecies at 1×10^{157}. In order to visualize this probability, Stone says we cannot use the silver dollar because it's much too large. Instead, we must try to visualize an electron, because the electron is the only unit of measurement small enough to help us visualize our probability of 1×10^{157}. In fact, it is so small that it takes 2.5×10^{15} of them laid in a single-file line, side by side, to form an inch.[39]

Stone says that if we were asked to count the electrons in this one-inch line, it would take us 19,000,000 years to count them. And that's only if we never went to bed and counted them all day and all night long, and at a steady pace of 250 per minute. If we counted one *cubic* inch of them at a steady pace of 250 per minute, it would take us 19,000,000 × 19,000,000 × 19,000,000 years, or 6.9×10^{21} years to count them. Now, Stone says, in order to visualize your chance of 1×10^{157}, imagine taking this number, picking and marking an electron, stirring the electrons up, and then blindfolding yourself and trying to pick the correct marked electron. Again, what are the chances you would pick the right one? Zero chances. This, Stone says, is the chance of any one person fulfilling just *forty-eight* Old Testament prophecies. Again, Jesus fulfilled 332.[40]

After Christian apologist Josh McDowell did a thorough investigation of the New Testament, he said, "After trying to shatter the historicity and validity of the Scriptures, I came to the conclusion that it is historically trustworthy. If one discards the Bible as being unreliable, then we must discard almost all literature of antiquity."[41] He's right. The New Testament isn't a fraud. It's the real deal!

Finally, let's look at a few related issues associated with the Bible.

Discussion Questions

1. What reasons have unbelievers given you for not believing the New Testament is reliable? How did you respond to them? How would you respond to them now?

2. Why do you think people outside the faith so readily accept literary works of antiquity such as Homer's *Iliad* and the works of Plato, which have much less manuscript support than the New Testament on every dimension, and not the New Testament?

3. What recent archeological discoveries have you heard publicized in the media lately? Do you think they are authentic? Why or why not?

4. What current books have you seen publicized that attempt to discredit the reliability of the New Testament? What are they saying? How is it inaccurate?

5. For what are the Old Testament messianic prophecies meant to serve? What are the implications of this?

Seven

Got Issues?

*I*t is common for people outside the faith to question why ancient documents like the gospels of Thomas, Mary, and Peter weren't included in the Bible. After all, these gospels were just as likely contenders as the gospels of Matthew, Mark, Luke, and John, right? Is it because they taint the Christian faith and Jesus as Lord while the other four don't? What about the Apocrypha? Why don't Protestants consider it to be inspired by God? Also, how can Christians say they have God's Word when there are so many different translations that use completely different words? If we are to be women who love God with our *minds* as well as our hearts, we need to be able to address these issues. First, how did the church decide which books should be included in the Bible and which ones should not?

How Was the Canon Decided?

In the early church, when Christians wanted to know how God wanted them to live out their lives as Christians, they didn't have one large, bound book called the *Bible* containing the New Testament to read. Instead, what they had was a bunch of ancient letters written on scrolls or parchment. How did the early church know which ancient letters were inspired by God and which ones were not? Determining the answer to this question is an issue of *canonicity*.

The word *canon* comes from the Greek word *kanon* and is a "rod, ruler, staff, or measure" that symbolizes the standard for something in ancient Greece. The early church took this concept and applied it to the ancient documents circulating in the church to help them *recognize* which ones were inspired by God. They were to dictate the norms or standards of faith (and practice) for the church. These documents are the books included in the New Testament we have today, and make up what is called the New Testament *canon*.

According to Geisler and Nix, assembling the canon was a three-step process. First, the ancient documents included in it were inspired by God. Second, the early church *recognized* which documents those were. Finally, the collection was preserved by God's people, the church.[1]

Notice that I said the church *recognized* which documents were inspired by God and not *decided* which were inspired by God. It's imperative that we understand that the early church didn't sit down at a council one day, lay a bunch of ancient documents out on a table, and take a vote on which documents they wanted to be considered inspired by God and therefore included in the New Testament (as Dan Brown's novel *The Da Vinci Code* would have us believe). Instead, they understood that God inspired certain writings, which gave them their authority, and that it was their job to recognize which documents those were. I like how Geisler and Nix put it. They say, "A book is valuable because it is inspired, and not inspired because men found it to be valuable."[2] Exactly! How then did the early church recognize which ancient documents were inspired by God and therefore authoritative and which ones were not? It used five criteria.

First, the documents must have been written either by an apostle, an associate of an apostle, or by someone who had proper apostolic authority, such as Jesus' brothers, James and Jude.

Some of you might be saying, "Hold on a minute." Weren't some of the letters included in the New Testament canon technically anonymous? If that's true, then how did the early church recognize which documents were written by an apostle, an associate of an apostle, or by someone who had proper apostolic authority, and which ones were not?

While it's true there weren't names on some of the New Testament documents, such as the four gospels, their authorship was nonetheless well established in tradition. What does that mean? It means that the leaders of the early church orally passed down the authorship of the authentic gospels to the next generation of church leaders, who then passed it down to the next, so that each successive generation would know which gospels were authentic and which ones were not. Why was this necessary?

Because heretical and forged counterfeit gospels started circulating as early as the late second century and were being posed as the authentic gospels. Therefore, to protect the identity of the genuine gospels, the early church leaders made sure that the next generation of church leaders knew for certain which documents were authentic and which ones were not.

Second, the authorship of the New Testament documents had to have been firmly grounded in the historical Christian tradition. In other words, there had to have been great confidence that the gospel of Luke was written by Paul's companion and physician, Dr. Luke, and that the gospel of John was written by the apostle John, and so on.

Third, the documents must have been written by a church leader of the first-generation church if it wasn't written by an apostle, an associate of an apostle, or by someone who had proper apostolic authority.

Fourth, the documents had to have been widely circulating among the local churches throughout the ancient world and had to have been universally accepted by the early church as documents written by apostles, associates of apostles, people with proper apostolic authority, or first-century church leaders.

Finally, the ideas and beliefs expressed in the documents had to reflect the ideas and beliefs of the apostles. For this reason, documents like the gospels of Peter, Thomas, and Mary weren't even candidates.

Next, what about the Apocrypha?

What Is the Apocrypha and Where Does It Fit In?

The Apocrypha is the fourteen (or fifteen, depending upon how they were divided) books that were written after the book of Malachi in the Old Testament, but before the book of Matthew in the New Testament. In classical and Hellenistic Greek, the word *Apocrypha* means "hidden" or "hard to understand." There is much controversy over their divine authority and whether or not they were, or should be, part of the canon.

According to Geisler and Nix, some scholars believe there were two canons in the ancient Near East. The first is the Palestinian Canon, which was the Hebrew canon recognized by the early Jews. This canon did *not* contain the apocryphal books.

The second is the so-called "Alexandrian Canon," which is a Greek arrangement that supposedly came out of Alexandria, Egypt, around the same time the Septuagint was made. This canon supposedly *did* contain the apocryphal books. Some scholars thought there were actually two canons—one that contained these extra books and one that didn't—because the earliest copies of the Septuagint contain some of the apocryphal books while the Hebrew canon did not.

Geisler and Nix insist, however, that there is no other evidence that the "Alexandrian Canon" existed. The only evidence to support this theory is that *some*, not all, of the apocryphal books were found in the earliest manuscripts of the Septuagint. While scholars continue to debate this issue, what's important for us, as women who want to love God with our minds as well as our hearts, is an understanding of some of the basic facts about the Apocrypha and where it stands today outside of this dispute.

First, the following is a list of the fifteen apocryphal books:

1. Book of Wisdom
2. Sirach
3. Tobit
4. Judith
5. 3 Esdras
6. 1 Maccabees
7. 2 Maccabees
8. Baruch (chapters 1–5)
9. Baruch (chapter 6)
10. 4 Esdras
11. Esther 10:4–16:24
12. Daniel 3:24–90
13. Daniel 13
14. Daniel 14
15. Prayer of Manasseh

Second, the apocryphal books were included in the Protestant Bible up until the nineteenth century. However, while it's true they once were included, what's also true is that they were placed in a section of their own because they weren't considered to have the same divine authority as the rest of the Old Testament books. Today, the Apocrypha is *not* included in the Protestant Bible and is *not* considered to have divine authority.

Third, in 1546, at the Council of Trent, the Roman Catholic Church declared eleven of the fourteen (or fifteen) apocryphal books canonical, rejecting 3 Esdras, 4 Esdras, and the Prayer of Manasseh. This still stands.

Fourth, notice that some of the apocryphal books are not actual books, but rather extra chapters of books. For example, chapter three in the book of Daniel in the Protestant Bible ends at verse thirty, but ends at verse ninety in the Roman Catholic Bible. Also, the book of Daniel ends with chapter twelve in the Protestant Bible, but ends at chapter fourteen in the Roman Catholic Bible. The same is true for the book of Esther. In the Protestant Bible, the book of Esther ends at chapter ten, verse three. In the Catholic Bible, it ends at chapter ten, verse ten. Therefore, when Protestants discuss the Bible with Catholics and hear Catholics talk about information unfamiliar to them, it's often because the Catholic is drawing from passages or books Protestants don't consider canonical. This is true for the doctrine of purgatory, which comes from 2 Maccabees 12:39–46, a book that is not a part of the Protestant canon.

Finally, Geisler and Nix point out the following additional facts about the Apocrypha:[3]

- It wasn't part of the Hebrew canon of the Jews.
- Josephus, the ancient Jewish historian, overtly excludes the Apocrypha when numbering the Old Testament Scriptures in his historical documentation.
- The Jamnia Jewish scholars in AD 90 didn't recognize the Apocrypha as canonical.
- Many of the patristic Fathers of the early church such as Origen, Cyril of Jerusalem, and Athanasius spoke out *against* the Apocrypha.
- Jerome, the famous translator of the Latin *Vulgate*, explicitly rejected the Apocrypha.
- Jesus and the apostles never quoted from it as Scripture—ever.
- Some of the apocryphal teachings are in direct conflict with other biblical passages, and therefore the Apocrypha is viewed as unbiblical and heretical.
- Most of it was written during the intertestamental period, or the four-hundred-year period known as the "The Dark Period" or "The Years of Silence," when God was silent and didn't inspire prophetic writers.
- Even many Roman Catholic scholars rejected it through the Reformation period.
- The acceptance of it at the Council of Trent was suspicious because scholars believe making it canonical was used as a counterattack against Luther.

- It was never fully accepted as canonical *even* by the Roman Catholic Church prior to 1546.

If the canon was recognized by the early church leaders and is closed, why are there so many different translations of the Bible today?

What Are the Differences Among the Modern Translations?

Growing up, the only version of the Bible I remember was the King James Version (KJV). It wasn't that others were not available, but it was the only version of the Bible my family owned, and the only version used by the church I grew up in. I hated reading it when I was a child because I couldn't understand it. It was totally incomprehensible to me.

Today, we have over sixty English translations available. But with so many choices comes much confusion, even among Christians. What are the differences among the modern translations of the Bible available today?

There are three different types of translations: (1) literal translation (or word-for-word), (2) dynamic equivalent translation (or meaning-to-meaning, or thought-for-thought), and (3) free translation (or paraphrase).

Literal Translations

Literal (or word-for-word) translations are the versions that most accurately reflect the original Hebrew, Aramaic, and Greek texts. Literal translations translate the Bible, keeping the exact wording and/or phrasing of the original text. This means that the Hebrew, Aramaic, and Greek syntax isn't changed to the English syntax.

In Spanish, adjectives come after the nouns they modify, not before, as they do in English. For instance, if I want to say "red purse" in Spanish, I would say, *bolso rojo*, which literally means "purse red." This is a literal translation. I have not changed the Spanish syntax to the English syntax when I translated the phrase. This is what literal translations do. They translate the original text word for word or phrase for phrase without changing the syntax, even if it doesn't make sense in the language it's translated into. For this reason, literal translations can sometimes be confusing. This is one of the reasons why I had such a hard time understanding the King James Version as a child. Many of the words were scrambled, and I found it incredibly frustrating to unscramble them and put them into their correct order. It was simply too much work. While it is true that reading literal translations can sometimes be tricky, literal translations are the very best versions to read when doing word studies.

Popular literal translations are:

- Interlinear Bible (German Bible Society and United Bible Studies/1967)[4]
- Geneva Bible (GB/1560)
- King James Version (KJV/1611)
- New King James Version (NKJV/1982)
- American Standard Version (ASV/1901)
- Revised Standard Version (RSV/1952, revised in 1971)
- New American Bible (NAB/1970, Psalms revised in 1996)
- New American Standard Bible (NASB/1971, revised in 1977 and 1995)
- New Revised Standard Version (NRSV/1990)
- English Standard Version (ESV/2001)
- Holman Christian Standard Bible (HCSB/2004)

Dynamic Equivalent Translations

Dynamic equivalent translations (or meaning-for-meaning, or thought-for-thought) are translations that change the syntax of the original language into the language it is being translated into, adding additional words and phrases if necessary. For instance, in a dynamic equivalent translation, the Spanish phrase *bolso rojo* would be translated into the phrase "red purse." Notice that I have not changed the meaning of the text. The meaning remains the same. What I did do, however, is unscramble the words into the English syntax so that it is more understandable in English. This is what dynamic equivalent translations do. They do not change the ideas or thoughts. Rather, they express the same thoughts using different words or phrases to communicate the same ideas.

It's important to note that dynamic equivalent translations *retain* as best they can the historical and sociopolitical context in which the biblical text was written. This is also true of literal translations. Sometimes, however, ideas and/or phrases simply aren't translatable. Therefore, sometimes biblical translators are forced to choose the next closest, understandable context to convey the information to modern-day readers.

Popular dynamic equivalent translations are:

- Jerusalem Bible (JB/1966)
- Good News Translation (GNT/1976, revised in 1992)
- New International Version (NIV/1978, revised in 1984 and in 2011)
- New Jerusalem Bible (NJB/1985)
- Revised English Bible (REB/1989)
- Good News Bible (GNB/1976, revised in 1992)
- New Living Translation (NLT/1996, revised in 2004)
- Today's New International Version (2005)

Free Translations

Finally, free translations (or paraphrases) are just that—free in their translation. They make no attempt to retain the original words, syntax, or even historical and sociopolitical context. In fact, free translations purposely seek to remove their readers from the Bible's historical and sociopolitical context. Essentially, they put the Bible in today's street language. Why would translators do such a thing? They do it so that their readers "get" the biblical text at a visceral level.

While there are some Christians who think free translations are blasphemous, I believe they have a very important place in our culture today. The first time I read Eugene Peterson's free translation, *The Message*, I was able to understand the emotional charge of many of Jesus' verbal exchanges with the Pharisees and Sadducees that I simply wasn't able to grasp reading other translations. I was able to "get" concepts I simply wasn't able to "get" before. This is why it's the *only* version I give to unbelievers who identify with the culture. It speaks their language. And when they read it, for the first time in their lives they see the Bible as relevant to their lives today, and not as the antiquated, outdated, and irrelevant book they initially thought it was. For many, it's a great stepping-stone.

Popular free translations or paraphrases are:

- The Living Bible (TLB/1971)
- The Message (2002)

It is also important to be aware of the following two divergent translations. These translations were translated by people and/or groups classified as cults. They are:

- New World Translation (NWT/1961, translated by The Watch Tower Bible and Tract Society, otherwise known as Jehovah's Witnesses)
- The Sacred Scriptures (SS/1961, translated by The Assemblies of Yahweh, and particularly their leader, Jacob O. Meyer)

When speaking at events, women often ask me what version is the "right" version to use. I never tell them, because there is no "right" version. Instead, I tell them what version is right for me. Choosing a translation of the Bible is very personal. Some people will only read literal translations, while others prefer one of the free translations. For the record, I like the NIV, the version I have used in this book. However, I also use several other versions. When I'm doing word studies, I use an interlinear Bible. When I'm leading seeker groups, I use *The Message*. When I'm speaking to older crowds or at traditional churches, I use the New King James Version. When I memorize Scripture, I use the NIV to keep what I memorize consistent.

When choosing which translation is right for you, it's important to know what the differences are among the various translations available today *before* you make your choice. Then select the translation that best fits your needs. Only you know what those are.

Once you make your choice, please respect the choices others make. Sadly, I've heard Christians who accuse other Christians of being "less spiritual" because they don't read the King James Version of the Bible, as if it were the only valid translation available. The King James Version is just one option among many great options. It is not the only "right" option. In Matthew 7:2–4, Jesus warns believers not to be hasty to judge others, for the same measure we use against them will be used against us. If we are to be women who love God with our hearts *and* our minds, we must respect the choices of others, just as we would want them to respect ours (Matt. 7:12).

Discussion Questions

1. What is the distinction between the church *recognizing* which ancient New Testament documents were inspired by God, and therefore part of the canon, and the church *deciding* which ones were?

2. How are Protestant and Catholic Bibles different? How might this affect their individual beliefs?

3. Do you think the Apocrypha should be a part of the canon? Why or why not?

4. What translation of the Bible do you use? How did you choose it? Why do you like it?

5. What are other advantages and disadvantages of the various translations of the Bible available today (literal translation, dynamic equivalent, and free translation)?

Part **3**

THE
CENTRAL
TRUTH

Eight

The Rolling Stone

The apostle Paul said if Jesus didn't rise from the dead, our preaching and our faith is useless and Christians are to be pitied above all people (1 Cor. 15:14, 19). The resurrection is the heart of the Christian faith. If Jesus didn't rise from the dead, then Jesus isn't who He said He was, there is no such thing as eternal life, and death wasn't defeated. This means that Christians will not be judged by the God of the universe, Christianity is false, and Christians are lost (1 Cor. 15:17).[1] The question is, is there any objective evidence to support the claim that Jesus rose from the dead, or is it a belief Christians must hold by faith? While atheists think the resurrection is nothing more than a myth, there are good reasons for believing it really happened. If we are to be women who love God with our hearts *and* our minds, it is crucial we know what those reasons are.

My favorite way to defend the resurrection is by using the Minimal Facts Approach developed by resurrection specialists Gary Habermas and Mike Licona.[2] It's simple, easy to remember, and effective.

Minimal Facts Approach

The Minimal Facts Approach takes five facts surrounding Jesus' death that are well verified in history and accepted as true by virtually all scholars who study the subject (including those most skeptical) and demonstrates why the best explanation for all the facts is that Jesus rose from the dead. The five facts are: (1) Jesus *died* by crucifixion, (2) Jesus' disciples really *believed* He rose from the dead, (3) Paul's dramatic conversion, (4) the skeptic James' conversion, and (5) the empty tomb.[3]

Fact 1: Jesus Died by Crucifixion

The first fact is that Jesus *died* by crucifixion. Is there any evidence to support this? Yes. First, all four gospels in the New Testament support it (Matt. 27:31; Mark 15:25; Luke 23:33; John 19:18). In addition, there are multiple dispassionate, non-Christian sources that support it as well. For instance, the Jewish historian Josephus said in his work *Antiquities*, "When Pilate, at the suggestion of the principal men among us, had condemned him to the cross. . . ."[4] Tacitus, the Roman historian, said that "Nero fastened the guilt [of the burning of Rome] and inflicted the most exquisite tortures on a class hated for their abominations, called Christians by the populace. Christus, from whom the name had its origin, suffered the extreme penalty during the reign of Tiberius at the hands of one of our procurators, Pontius Pilate."[5] And Lucian, the Greek satirist, said, "The Christians, you know, worship a man to this day—the distinguished personage who introduced their novel rites, and was crucified on that account."[6] The Stoic philosopher Mara Bar-Serapion and the Talmud also supported it.[7]

That Jesus *died* by crucifixion is a well-documented historical fact. Nobody who studies the subject inside or outside the faith believes He didn't. The fact is too well-documented.

Common Objections

Some of you may be saying, "But wait a minute. Unbelievers won't accept the Gospels as credible evidence because they don't view the Bible as God's inspired and inerrant word." They don't have to. All they have to do is view the Scriptures as a collection of ancient documents written by first-century historians who accurately recorded the events surrounding Jesus' birth, life, ministry, and death. If they won't accept the Gospels on those terms, educate them that archeology and historians *outside* the faith also confirm the historical accounts they recorded. Therefore, they should be accepted as the accurate historical documents that they are.

But some say maybe Jesus didn't really die on the cross. Maybe He just fainted and then regained consciousness when He was laid in the cool, dark tomb so that it looked like He came back from the dead, when in reality He never died in the first place. This objection is called the *Swoon Theory* or the *Apparent Death Theory*.

While the average person on the streets still brings the Swoon Theory up as an objection to this fact, no credible scholars today even acknowledge it as a viable objection for one very important reason: There is no way Jesus didn't *die,* given the nature of scourging and crucifixion and the credentials of the Roman executioners who crucified Jesus.

The Gospels record that before Jesus was crucified, the Roman guards first scourged Him, most likely giving Him thirty-nine lashes, one less than the maximum sentence allowed (Deut. 25:1–3). What was it like? The Journal of the American Medical Association (JAMA) says of the practice:

> The usual instrument was a short whip . . . with several single or braided leather thongs of variable lengths, in which small iron balls or sharp pieces of sheep bones were tied at intervals . . . the man was stripped of his clothing, and his hands were tied to an upright post. . . . The back, buttocks, and legs, were flogged. . . . The scourging . . . was intended to weaken the victim to a state just short of collapse or death. . . . As the Roman soldiers repeatedly struck the victim's back with full force, iron balls would cause deep contusions, and the leather thongs and sheep bones would cut into the skin and subcutaneous tissues. Then, as the flogging continued, the lacerations would tear into the underlying skeletal muscles.[8]

Given the nature of Roman scourging, it's a wonder Jesus didn't die from the scourging alone. And Jesus endured this brutal beating *before* He was hung on the cross.

You might think Jesus handled the scourging better than the average person. But He didn't. We know from the gospel accounts that a Roman soldier had to recruit a man named Simon from the crowd to carry Jesus' cross to Golgotha because Jesus was so weakened by the scourging that He couldn't carry it (Matt. 27:32; Mark 15:21).

Some have said that maybe the Roman guards thought He was dead and took Him off the cross before He was dead. This is also unlikely. In ancient Rome, crucifixion was the method of capital punishment used by the Romans to execute the lower class, slaves, soldiers, the extremely violent, and people accused of treason. Crucifixion was the Romans' favorite method of execution because it not only ensured that its victims died a slow and agonizing death but it also was used as a reminder to passersby where disobedience to Rome ultimately led.

Not only was the method the Romans' favorite, they were superb at it. Nobody left the cross alive. And to ensure no one did, the Roman guards often broke the legs of the convicts who hung on the crosses to speed up their deaths. This was done because when people are crucified, they die of asphyxiation because hanging on the cross puts pressure on the lungs and collapses them, making it difficult to breathe. The victims use their legs to push up and take a breath. However, over time, they become exhausted and suffocate to death.

To facilitate the process, the Roman guards broke the legs of their prisoners. Did they do this to Jesus? We know from John 19:33 that the Roman guards didn't have to. Jesus was already dead when they approached, just as was prophesized in Psalm 34:20. And just to make sure, the gospel of John tells us that a Roman guard pierced His side with a spear (John 19:34).

The Roman guards who crucified felons on death row were masters at their job. They crucified people for a living. They knew when people were dead and when they weren't. They also knew that if they accidentally took someone off the cross before that criminal was dead, they paid for their mistake with their own lives. This served as a huge incentive to make sure mistakes were not made.

When Jesus was crucified, the Roman guards made sure Jesus was dead *before* they took Him down from the cross. And given the credentials of the Roman guards who were given the incentives they were, there is no way they made a mistake when they crucified Jesus, especially since Jesus was such a high-profile case. Jesus died by crucifixion. Of that there is no doubt. As skeptic John Dominic Crossan said, "That he [Jesus] was crucified is as sure as anything historical can ever be."[9]

Fact 2: Jesus' Disciples Believed He Rose From the Dead

The second fact is that Jesus' twelve disciples really *believed* Jesus rose from the dead. Is there any evidence to support this? Yes. First, the apostle Paul wrote about it. How would Paul know what the disciples believed? Paul knew what they believed because he spent time with them. In Galatians 1:18, Paul said that three years after his conversion, he went to Jerusalem to become acquainted with Peter (Cephas). He also saw James. In addition, he spent time with James, John, and Peter together, the three that made up Jesus' inner circle (Gal. 2:9). Paul knew what the apostles believed because when he spent time with them, they told him what they believed. Therefore, what Paul recorded about their beliefs is trustworthy.

Next, according to Habermas and Licona, the church's earliest oral creeds record the disciples belief about the resurrection as well. What are the earliest oral creeds? They are the creeds embedded in the New Testament that date as early as AD 50, making them the earliest sources speaking of Jesus' resurrection. Before the details of Jesus' life were ever written down in the New Testament, the first generation of Christians verbally repeated the significant facts about His life, such as the resurrection, in the form of a creed, so that these facts that were passed down to them by the disciples could be accurately preserved. First Corinthians 15:3–5 is such an oral creed. It says: "For what I received I passed on to you as of first importance: that Christ died for our sins according to the Scriptures, that he was buried, that he was raised on the third day according to the Scriptures, and that he appeared to Cephas, and then to the Twelve."

In this creed, the first generation of Christians clearly professes that Jesus rose from the dead. This means that the belief Jesus' disciples passed on to them was that the disciples truly believed Jesus rose from the dead. How do we know this text is one of the early church's oral creeds and not just information Paul added? According to Habermas and Licona, we know it's a creed because Paul used the word *received* to introduce the text, which is an indicator that the information to follow was not his own, but rather information he received from an outside source. In addition, that Paul used the word *passed* suggests that he was purposely passing along to others the information he received. Gary Habermas says, "That this confession is an early Christian, pre-Pauline creed is recognized by virtually all critical scholars across a very wide theological spectrum."[10] There is no doubt from this early oral creed that the disciples truly believed Jesus rose from the dead.

Finally, the strongest evidence that Jesus' disciples really *believed* He rose from the dead is that their characters were utterly transformed, so much so that eleven out of Twelve were willing to die for their beliefs, ten of whom did. Prior to Jesus' death, the apostles were known to question Jesus, and in the end deserted Him (Matt. 26:56). However, after Jesus rose from the dead and they saw Him, they became entirely different men. Suddenly they weren't afraid to preach that Jesus rose from the dead, as proof to anyone who would listen that He was the Jewish Messiah. Nothing could stop them. Not admonishment. Not jail. Not even death.[11] The only two apostles who weren't killed for their belief were Judas Iscariot (who killed himself for betraying Jesus) and John (who was exiled on the Island of Patmos for his belief). If the apostles didn't really believe Jesus rose from the dead, you would think at least one of them would have cracked under pressure and recanted to save himself. Yet none of them did. The only logical explanation for the change in the apostles' character and behavior is that they really *believed* they saw Jesus alive again after His death.

Common Objections

Unbelievers are quick to point out that many people die for their beliefs. This proves nothing. All one has to do is look at the Islamic jihadists to know this is true. Yes, but people don't usually die for a lie. The Islamic terrorists are willing to die for beliefs they *believe* are true, no matter how misguided we believe they may be. But they aren't dying for something they know is a lie. If Jesus' apostles didn't really believe that Jesus died and rose from the dead, because they were running some kind of social or political scam and hid His body, they wouldn't have been willing to die, because they would have known that Jesus didn't really come back from the dead. If it was all a sham, it's unlikely that all of them would have been willing to die anyway. As the apostles started being brutally executed, you would think at least one of them would have produced Jesus' body, if that were possible, to save his own skin. Of course, no one ever did.[12] Again, the only reasonable explanation for the apostles' radical character and behavioral change is that they believed they saw Jesus alive again.

Fact 3: Paul's Dramatic Conversion

The third fact is Paul's dramatic conversion. As Paul was on the road to Damascus, headed to persecute Christians, he claimed to see the resurrected Jesus. This encounter transformed Paul from a cruel Jewish Pharisee into a gentle man who loved Jesus (and Christians) more than life itself. Is there any evidence to support this? Yes. The apostle Paul tells us about his dramatic conversion himself.

First, Paul tells us what he was like *before* his conversion. In 1 Corinthians 15:9, Paul says, "For I am the least of the apostles and do not even deserve to be called an apostle, because I persecuted the church of God." In Galatians 1:13, he says, "For you have heard of my previous way of life in Judaism, how intensely I persecuted the church of God and tried to destroy it."

Then Paul tells us what he was like *after* his conversion. In Galatians 1:15–16, he says, "But when God, who set me apart from my mother's womb and called me by his grace, was pleased to reveal his Son in me so that I might preach among the Gentiles. . . ." And in Galatians 1:22–23, he says, "I was personally unknown to the churches of Judea that are in Christ. They only heard the report: 'The man who formerly persecuted us is now preaching the faith he once tried to destroy.'"

The question is "What changed Paul?" For the answer, we need to look at Paul' testimony. When Paul told Festus that he would like to appeal his case to Caesar, as was his right as a Roman citizen, Paul told King Agrippa what happened. He said:

> I was so obsessed with persecuting them that I even hunted them down in foreign cities. On one of these journeys I was going to Damascus with the authority and commission of the chief priests. About noon, King Agrippa, as I was on the road, I saw a light from heaven, brighter than the sun, blazing around me and my companions. We all fell to the ground, and I heard a voice saying to me in Aramaic, "Saul, Saul, why do you persecute me? It is hard for you to kick against the goads."
> Then I asked, "Who are you, Lord?"
> "I am Jesus, whom you are persecuting," the Lord replied.
>
> Acts 26:11–15

Paul makes it clear that the cause behind his radical conversion was that he truly *believed* he saw the risen Jesus while traveling on the road to Damascus (1 Cor. 9:1). And as a result, Paul was never the same again. And like the other apostles, Paul wasn't afraid to tell anyone who would listen what happened to him. And like the other apostles, Paul too was willing to die for this belief and did. Paul was beheaded in AD 64.

In addition to Paul's testimony, Paul's dramatic conversion was also documented in the writings of Clement of Rome, Polycarp, Tertullian, Dionysius of Corinth, and Origen.

Common Objections

But, a skeptic might say, people change religions all the time. Yes, they do. However, what makes Paul's conversion unique is what *caused* him to change his religion. Unlike people today who hop around from one religion to another because others are doing it, or because they think it makes them look politically correct, Paul changed his religion because he really *believed* he saw and heard the resurrected Jesus. Paul's belief was extremely unpopular and definitely not politically correct. And very few were following this belief. Paul's reason did not follow a trend. It sent him to his death.

That the apostle Paul had a radical conversion because he truly *believed* he saw the risen Jesus on the road to Damascus is a well-documented fact in history.

Fact 4: The Skeptic James' Conversion

The fourth fact is that Jesus' brother James, who was first a skeptic, converted to Christianity because he too *believed* he saw Jesus resurrected from the dead. Is there any evidence to support this? Yes, there is.

While the New Testament text doesn't explicitly say that James was a skeptic, what it does say about James' belief prior to his conversion leads us to conclude he was. When Jesus was teaching in a crowded house, the Bible says that Jesus' family heard about it and went to confront Him. The gospel of Mark tells us that his family said He was out of his mind (Mark 3:21) and the gospel of John says that "even his own brothers did not believe in him" (John 7:5). And who were his brothers? They were James, Jude, and Simon. These passages make it clear that no one in Jesus' family (except his mother) believed Jesus was who He claimed He was, including James. Gary Habermas says, "That James was an unbeliever during Jesus' public ministry is granted by almost all contemporary scholars."[13]

At the same time, however, the New Testament also talks about James' leadership of the Jerusalem church (Acts 15:12–21; Gal. 1:19). Again, the question is "What happened to James that made him convert from a skeptic to a church leader?" The apostle Paul tells us. It's the same thing that happened to Paul—James really *believed* Jesus appeared to him after His death (1 Cor. 15:3–7).

And Paul wasn't the only one who said it. People outside the faith documented it as well, such as Josephus and Hegesippus.[14]

That Jesus' brother James converted from a skeptic to the leader of the Jerusalem church because he truly *believed* Jesus appeared to him after He was crucified is a well-documented fact in history. And like the twelve apostles and the apostle Paul, James too was willing to die for this belief and did. James was also beheaded.

Fact 5: The Empty Tomb

The last fact is that the tomb Jesus was buried in was empty.[15] According to Habermas and Licona, this fact, however, is different from the other four facts in that it doesn't meet the two requirements for being a minimal fact. Like the others, it's a fact that is well-documented in history. However, according to Habermas and Licona, it isn't accepted as true by every scholar who studies the subject: It's only accepted by 75 percent of them. However, they say the evidence is still strong enough to include it as an essential fact.[16] There are three arguments for the empty tomb. They can be easily remembered by the acronym J.E.T., which stands for Jerusalem Factor, Enemy Attestation, and Testimony of Women.[17] Let's look at the Jerusalem Factor first.

The *Jerusalem Factor* states that (1) because Jesus was publicly executed in Jerusalem, and (2) because Jerusalem was where Jesus was buried and where His tomb was reported as empty, and (3) because Jerusalem was where Jesus first appeared to people after He was crucified, it would have been impossible for Christianity to get off the ground as a new religion in Jerusalem if Jesus' body was still in the tomb there. All Jesus' Jewish enemies and/or the Roman government would have had to do was simply take Jesus' dead body from the tomb and publicly display it for all to see. But they never did. There are no reports in the historical accounts that this ever happened. Josephus didn't report it, nor did Tacitus, Lucian, Celsus, or Hegesippus. If Jesus' tomb wasn't empty despite the claim that it was, surely *someone* would have documented it. Yet no one did.

Enemy Attestation states that even Jesus' enemies claimed Jesus' tomb was empty. In fact, both Christian and non-Christian sources state that Jesus' enemies accused Jesus' disciples of stealing His body to account for why the tomb was empty. The gospel of Matthew states this (Matt. 28:12–13), as do the writings of Justin Martyr, Trypho (108), and Tertullian (*De Spectaculis* 30). Jesus' enemies would never have accused the disciples of stealing Jesus' dead body if the tomb wasn't empty. They had no ulterior motive for doing so. In fact, because they were Jesus' enemies, they would have liked nothing more than to produce Jesus' dead body to stop Christianity from growing. But they couldn't, because they didn't know where it was. This is why they accused the disciples of stealing it. The tomb was empty. And even Jesus' enemies acknowledged this.

Finally, let's look at the *Testimony of Women*. All four gospels report that it was the women in Jesus' life, and not the men, who first reported that Jesus' tomb was empty. If the gospel writers invented the story of the empty tomb to purposely deceive others, they would have never said that women were the first to discover it, because women weren't viewed as credible witnesses in Jewish culture during that time. The Jewish Talmud said, "Any evidence which a woman [gives] is not valid, also they are not valid to offer. This is equivalent to saying that one who is rabbinically accounted a robber is qualified to give the same evidence as a woman" (Rosh Hashanah 1.8). The works of Josephus echoed this. He said, "But let not the testimony of women be admitted, on account of the levity and boldness of their sex, nor let servants be admitted to give testimony on account of the ignobility of their soul; since it is probable that they may not speak truth, either out of hope of gain, or fear of punishment" (*Antiquities* 4.8.15).

If the disciples invented the story that the tomb was empty, they would have named witnesses who would be credible in the eyes of the Jews. They would have said men like Joseph of Arimathea or Nicodemus found the empty tomb, not women. The reason they didn't is because the story is true. Jesus' tomb was empty, and it was the women in Jesus' life, and not the men, who discovered it.

Common Objections

Some might argue that the tomb wasn't actually empty. Perhaps the disciples (or the women) went to the wrong tomb and erroneously concluded that Jesus rose from the dead. There is no way this could have happened. If the disciples did go to the wrong tomb, the Jewish officials and/or the Roman guards would have been more than happy to point them in the right direction. Everyone knew where the tomb was. And even in the very unlikely event they didn't, Joseph of Arimathea would have known. It was in his tomb that Jesus was buried.

But maybe someone other than the disciples stole Jesus' body. This is also unlikely because it doesn't explain Paul's or James' conversion, or why the apostles believed they saw Jesus alive after His death. All it explains is the empty tomb, none of the other facts.

Despite what 25 percent of scholars believe today, there are more reasons than not to believe Jesus' tomb was empty.

Evaluating the Facts

For a theory to be viable, it must be able to adequately explain all the facts, not just some of them. For instance, while claiming someone stole Jesus' body may explain why the tomb was empty, it doesn't explain the apostles' radical behavioral change, or Paul's or James' conversions. Likewise, if Jesus' disciples lied and hid Jesus' body, it doesn't explain the conversions of Paul or James, who claim they saw Jesus resurrected from the dead.[18]

Therefore, if people put forth alternative theories when you are defending the resurrection to them, determine whether or not the alternative theories being suggested explain all five facts. If they fail to explain even one of them, they are not viable options. All five facts happened. All five facts must be adequately explained. There is no way around this. According to Habermas and Licona, when all five facts surrounding Jesus' death are considered, the best explanation for them is that Jesus rose from the dead, just as the Bible says He did. The late Adrian Rogers once said, "The resurrection is not merely important to the historic Christian faith;

without it, there would be no Christianity. It is the singular doctrine that elevates Christianity above all other world religions."[19] He's right. It's not just a matter of a rolling stone. It's a matter of life or death—literally.

Discussion Questions

1. Why is the resurrection the central truth of the Christian faith?

2. In your own words, explain the Minimal Facts Approach.

3. How would you explain to unbelievers the approach they should take to the New Testament when citing it as evidence?

4. What other objections have you heard in the past about each of the five facts? How did you respond? How would you respond now?

5. How is the apostles' willingness to die for their belief that Jesus rose from the dead different from the radical Islamic jihadists who are dying for their beliefs today?

Part **4**

THE
REAL
WORLD

Nine

Through the Looking Glass

Once upon a time, there were two little girls who dreamed about becoming concert pianists. Their favorite thing to do was close their eyes and envision themselves playing Chopin's *Polonaise in A Major* on the Steinway concert grand at Carnegie Hall. They could actually hear the music playing in their heads as their fingers ran up and down the keyboard with perfect agility and precision, delivering each melodic line energetically and expressively. Afterward, when they imagined taking a bow, they smiled in their minds as their audiences stood and erupted in thunderous applause.

Alice, the daughter of a plumber and a third-grade teacher, who was raised in America's heartland, diligently practiced the piano every day in pursuit of her dream. She practiced on an upright Baldwin her parents had saved up to buy for her. Before she practiced, she prayed God would help her play to the best of her ability. Every time she practiced, her parents told her how great she sounded and praised God for giving Alice this incredible gift. They marveled at how Alice, a beloved child of God, created in His image, could play at such a high level. Because they believed

God gave her this gift, they encouraged her to keep practicing, took her to concerts, and hired the best piano teachers they could afford. When Alice played in recitals and competitions, she reminded herself of Philippians 4:13, that she could do all things through Christ who gave her strength. When performances went well, she thanked God. When they didn't, she asked God what He wanted her to learn from the experience. When it was time for Alice to apply to colleges, her parents encouraged her to apply to Juilliard, reminding her of God's promise in Matthew 19:26 that all things are possible with God. They truly believed God would provide financially if Juilliard was God's plan for Alice's life. Her dream became a reality. At twenty-five, she performed at Carnegie Hall shortly after graduating from Juilliard. Today, Alice plays all over the world, delighting her listeners with every performance she gives. No performances, however, have ever been as memorable as the time she played for her grandmother's funeral, knowing her grandmother was with the Lord. In her free time, she plays at her church, worshiping and praising God. She also plays at orphanages, instilling dreams in others.

Sophie, the daughter of a bond trader and a clinical psychologist, who was raised on the upper east side of Manhattan, also diligently practiced the piano every day in pursuit of her dream. She practiced on the family's Bechstein concert grand that once belonged to her great-grandfather. When she did, she hoped she could play to the best of her ability. While she practiced, her parents repeatedly reminded her not to put so much time and effort into the "hobby" and were careful not to encourage her foolish dream. They wondered how Sophie, a daughter of theirs, could have evolved in such a way that she always had her head in the clouds. Because they believed the piano was a distraction from their goal of Sophie's pursuing a law degree, they scheduled math tutors during her practice time, rarely took her to concerts, and only hired piano teachers who were on board with their goals for Sophie's life. When Sophie played in recitals and competitions, she reminded herself she had to trust in her talent and ability. When performances went well, she praised herself. When they didn't, she berated herself. No performances would ever be as hard as when she played at her grandmother's funeral, because it was a reminder that she would never see her grandmother again. When it was time for Sophie to apply to colleges, Sophie's parents told her to apply to Harvard, where they had studied. They truly believed if Sophie was to get ahead in this rat race, Harvard was where she needed to be. At twenty-five, Sophie performed her first acquisition at a high-powered law firm in lower Manhattan shortly after graduating from Harvard Law School. Today, Sophie buys companies all over the world, delighting her bosses with every acquisition she makes. In her free time, she works even harder in hopes of becoming the youngest partner in the firm. Sophie's parents' dream became a reality. But Sophie's didn't. Nowadays, the only keyboard anyone hears Sophie play is the computer keyboard in her spacious, art deco, forty-fourth-floor office with a spectacular view.

Two girls. One dream. Two very different outcomes. What made the difference? Talent? Focus? Dedication? It was none of those things. Alice and Sophie came from two different worlds with two very different families and outlooks on life. And you might say it made a world of difference.

Worldviews

Alice and Sophie had what philosophers call different *worldviews*. "What in the world is a worldview?" Derived from the German word *Weltanschauung*, *welt* meaning "world," and *anschauung* meaning "outlook" or "view," a worldview is the mental lens through which one sees the world. Worldviews are like "glasses" that form the "interpretive" lenses that help people "make sense of life." They are our perceptions of the world and our place in it. Worldviews answer life's most important questions, such as:

- Who am I?
- What am I?
- Where am I?
- How did I get here?

- How am I supposed to live?
- How do I know what I know?
- How should I understand our world's history and its future direction?
- What should be important to me?

Where do worldviews come from?

They are inherited. As philosopher Patrick J. Hurley says, "Beginning in infancy, our worldview emerges quietly and unconsciously from enveloping influences such as culture, language, gender, religion, politics, and socioeconomic status. As we grow older, it continues to develop through the shaping forces of education and experience."[1] Worldviews sound like beliefs, don't they?

Like beliefs, worldviews reflect the sum total of who we are. However, worldviews are different from beliefs in that they are comprised of all the beliefs we hold that affect how we see the world. A belief stands alone. A single belief is not a worldview. But all of our beliefs knitted together are. Therefore, like beliefs, worldviews also direct our behaviors, which dramatically affect our lives, as you saw were the cases with Alice and Sophie. Plus, like beliefs, worldviews either help us see reality more clearly or they distort it.

Everyone has a worldview whether or not they realize it. I have a worldview. You have a worldview. If you are married, your husband has a worldview. If you have children, your children have worldviews that have been handed down and shaped by you and your husband. If you have grandchildren, your grandchildren's worldviews have likewise been influenced by and passed down from you and your children. As Christians, the question we need to ask ourselves is "How coherent is our worldview?"

Determining the answer to this question is the goal of this chapter. In it, we will examine the basic elements of the ten most common worldviews. At the same time, we will look at how each worldview answers eight of life's most important questions. Next, we will examine how Christless worldviews are passed on to us through what I call the new oral tradition. Finally, we will discuss how, as Christians, we should interact with our culture to equip us to successfully engage in our culture without contaminating our Christian theistic worldview.

While there are different ways to categorize worldviews, I like to classify them in relation to a person's view of God (theological) and to a specific system of thought (philosophical).

Theological Worldviews

Theism

The first theological worldview is *theism*. Theists believe in a personal, intelligent, infinite God, who created the universe out of nothing (*ex nihilo*). Theists believe God is present both outside the universe (transcendent) as well as inside the universe (immanent), but not a part of the universe. Theists also believe in miracles. In addition, they believe God is sovereign (in control of the universe and all its events) and who sometimes intervenes in the world's affairs via miracles. The three religions that hold to a theistic worldview are Christianity, Judaism, and Islam.

I'm not going to state the basic beliefs of these three religions because doing so goes beyond the scope of this book. However, I am going to state how both Christianity and Islam answer eight of the most important questions in life, to help us get a sense of how each worldview answers them. When answering them for the Islamic worldview, I will not differentiate between Sunni and Shiite beliefs, but will answer the questions generally.

CHRISTIANITY

1. **Who am I?**

   I am a child of God created in God's image.[2] Therefore, I have infinite value.[3]

2. **What am I?**

   I am both a material body and an immaterial soul.[4] When I die, my physical body decays, but my immaterial soul (which houses my intellect, will, and emotions) goes to be with the Lord in heaven where I have eternal life.

3. Where am I?

I am in a universe God spoke into existence out of nothing (*ex nihilo*). It is my temporary home.

4. How did I get here?

God created me and put me here.

5. How am I supposed to live?

I am supposed to live according to God's laws and precepts so that my life glorifies and honors Him in all I think, say, and do.

6. How do I know what I know?

I know what I know through God. God is the ultimate truth, and as such, has revealed it to me through the Bible (Special Revelation) and creation (General Revelation). Because truth is grounded in the very nature of God, truth is objective, knowable, universal, absolute, and unchanging. I use my mind (reason) and the laws of logic to understand revelation, and I understand science in light of Scripture, not Scripture in light of science.

7. How should I understand our world's history and its future direction?

The Bible tells me that God is sovereign and is responsible for the world's beginning, purpose, and end. The history of the world unfolds in the following five stages: Creation, Fall, Redemption, Glorification, and New Creation. God will bring destruction to the world as we know it on a cataclysmic level so it has an apocalyptic end.

8. What should be important to me?

Loving God with my heart, soul, and mind, and loving others as I love myself, should be important to me. I should also tell others about Christ, so they too can be reconciled to God and live with Him in eternity.

ISLAM

1. Who am I?

I am a creation of Allah and a descendant of Adam, whose nature was *not* changed by sin. I was born innocent and am

158

inherently good. Therefore, I am able to obey Allah completely and fully. However, I am a frail and forgetful human being who has a hard time obeying Allah.

2. **What am I?**
I am a material body and an immaterial soul. When I die, my physical body decays, but my immaterial soul, which houses my intellect, will, and emotions, either goes to paradise or hell.

3. **Where am I?**
I am in a universe Allah created in six days, which is my temporary home.

4. **How did I get here?**
Allah created me and put me here.

5. **How should I live?**
I should live my life in full submission to Allah's will because the word *Islam* means "submission," and the term *Muslim* means "one who submits." I should also faithfully do the following five pillars of Islam.

- *Shahadah* ("*There is no god but Allah. Muhammad is the messenger of Allah.*")
- *Salat* (prayer, five times daily)
- *Zakat* (almsgiving)
- *Sawm* (Ramadan fast, celebrating the advent of the Qur'an)
- *Hajj* (Mecca pilgrimage, commemorating Abraham)

I should also help bring Allah's will forth in the world by doing whatever it takes to bring infidels (unbelievers) into full submission to Allah's will.

6. **How do I know what I know?**
I know what I know through the Qur'an, which is Allah's final revelation to man. I believe the Qur'an is the word of Allah and was given to Gabriel, which was then transmitted to Muhammad.

7. **How should I understand our world's history and its future direction?**

I should understand world history as being under the complete control of Allah, whose will is to bring the entire world under Islamic control and Sharia Law.

8. **What should be important to me?**
What's important to me is living a sinless life and faithfully doing the five pillars of faith and other good works to please Allah and to earn my salvation and a place in paradise.

Like Christians, not all Muslims believe the same things. And not all Muslims are militant and wish to commit Jihad. However, despite the differences in views among Muslims, the above is the authoritative position of the Qur'an, whether or not Muslims believe it or adhere to it.

Deism

The second theological worldview is *deism*. Deists believe in a personal, intelligent, and infinite god who created the world out of nothing (*ex nihilo*) and governs it through the unchanging, eternal, natural laws of the universe. Deists also believe God is only outside the universe (transcendent), not inside the universe (immanent). Therefore, deists believe God is no longer involved in the world or its events. For deists, all they can know about God is what they glean about Him from the world. In addition, deists affirm the big miracle of creation out of nothing (*ex nihilo*), but deny smaller miracles like Jesus turning wine into water (John 2:1–11). Deists also deny man has access to God through religion, as well as deny all religious scriptures are revelations from God. Furthermore, deists deny that Jesus and the Holy Spirit are God and therefore reject the Trinity. For deists, all knowledge about the world, truth, and morality is obtained through reason, logic, and science. Moreover, deists believe human behavior is the cause of evil in the world, and blames it on the abuse or neglect inflicted by others. Some deists believe in some kind of afterlife while others do not. In deism, God is the Great Watchmaker who made the watch and is now watching it wind down. It is important to understand that deists vary in their beliefs, just as Christians and Muslims do.

1. **Who am I?**
   I am an animal who evolved from lower animal forms. I have no eternal value.
2. **What am I?**
   I am only a material body, which houses my intellect, will, and emotions. When I die, I will no longer exist. However, I might exist on some level in some kind of afterlife, but it's unclear what kind of life that might be or how it could happen.
3. **Where am I?**
   I am in a universe God created, but one in which He never intervenes.
4. **How did I get here?**
   I got here by evolution and natural selection.
5. **How should I live?**
   I should live my life to be happy, since my life on earth is the only life I have.
6. **How do I know what I know?**
   I know what I know (truth and morality) by reason, the laws of logic, and science.
7. **How should I understand our world's history and its future direction?**
   I should understand that our world's history and its future direction is determined by man and the natural laws of the universe as discovered by science.
8. **What should be important to me?**
   My personal happiness should be important to me.

Atheism

The third theological worldview is *atheism*. Atheists believe that no god of any kind, finite or infinite, exists. Some atheists believe the world popped into existence out of nothing while others believe it evolved from matter that always existed. In addition, atheists believe man is an animal that evolved through the process of evolution and natural selection. For the atheist, morals and values are determined by each person and therefore are relative or situational (dictated by the situation in which one finds oneself). Moreover, atheists believe evil exists, and state it as the main reason for not believing God exists.

There are four types of atheism. The first is *Dogmatic Atheism,* or traditional atheism, which denies that God exists. Dogmatic atheists say God never existed and never will, and believe any concept of God is nothing more than a "delusion" of man's mind. The second is called *Defensive Atheism,* which denies the *belief* in God. For the defensive atheist, God is nothing more than a belief one chooses to hold, similar to those a child holds when she believes in Santa Claus, unicorns, leprechauns, and fairies. The third type is called *Practical Atheism.* Practical atheists say they believe in God. However, they live their lives in contradiction to that belief. Finally, the fourth type is called *New Atheism.* New atheists are dogmatic and believe no God of any kind exists. They are different from the dogmatic atheist, however, in that they actively and aggressively seek to convince all non-atheists—people of faith, in particular—that God does not exist. As CNN journalist Simon Hooper correctly points out in his article "The Rise of the 'New Atheists,'" for the new atheist, "religion should not simply be tolerated, but should be countered, criticized, and exposed by rational argument wherever its influences arise."[5] New Atheism is the position heralded by the outspoken Richard Dawkins, the late Christopher Hitchens, Sam Harris, and Daniel Dennett. In an attempt to proclaim to the city of London that God doesn't exist, the new atheists plastered signs on London's famous red double-decker buses that read: "There's probably no God. Now stop worrying and enjoy your life." All atheists agree God doesn't exist. However, they may disagree on everything else.[6]

1. **Who am I?**
   I am an animal that evolved from lower animal forms. I have no eternal value.

2. What am I?

I am only a material body, which houses my intellect, will, and emotions. When I die, I will no longer exist.

3. Where am I?

I am in a purposeless universe that either popped into existence out of nothing or organized from uncreated, eternal matter.

4. How did I get here?

I got here by chance random forces, evolution, and natural selection.

5. How should I live?

I should live my life to be happy, since my life on earth is the only life I have.

6. How do I know what I know?

I know what I know (truth and morality) through reason, the laws of logic, and science.

7. How should I understand our world's history and its future direction?

I should understand that our world's history and its future direction are determined by man and the natural laws of the universe as discovered by science.

8. What should be important to me?

My personal happiness should be important to me.

Pantheism

The fourth theological worldview is *pantheism*. Pantheists believe the following different things about God:

- Everything in the physical world is God.
- God is absolute reality.
- God manifests in different forms (spirit, earth, air, water, fire, sun, moon, stars).
- God is like a force that permeates all things.
- God is mind.

Whatever pantheists believe about God, however, they all agree on two things: (1) God is impersonal, and (2) God is unknowable. Therefore, if pantheists pray, they are praying to an impersonal, unknowable force. For this reason, praying doesn't make sense for the pantheist. Pantheists also believe God did not create the world. Instead, they believe the world came forth from God himself (*ex Deo*). Because the world is God, it is worthy of worship.

However, Mary Baker Eddy, the founder of Christian Science, as well as some Hindus, believe the world is just an illusion (doctrine called *maya*). For them, since the world doesn't exist, neither does pain, suffering, evil, or death. The only way these things are overcome is realizing everything, including ourselves, is God.

For those who believe the world is God, God is inside the world (immanent), but not outside the world (transcendent).[7] Therefore, there can't be supernatural events like miracles. However, there can be supernormal events like channeling and some forms of healing.

Pantheists also deny that truth and morals are absolute, but strive to live moral lives according to what they believe is moral. In particular, they believe in developing themselves, being self-reliant, cooperative, and nonviolent. They also believe in preserving the world's natural resources. Morality, and good and evil, are irrelevant. However, once the pantheist realizes she is God, as God, good and evil are categories she has transcended. Hinduism, Taoism, some kinds of Buddhism, Scientology, Christian Science, Unity, and New Age Religions, including Wicca, are pantheistic religions.

Since pantheists believe a wide range of things, I will answer eight of their life's most important questions generally.

1. **Who am I?**
   I am God.

2. **What am I?**
   I am either only a physical body or only a mind who will one day realize I am God. If I do, when I die, I will be absorbed into the universe.

3. **Where am I?**

I am in a world that "eternally emanated" from God (*ex Deo*) *if* the world exists.

4. **How did I get here?**

I got here by evolution and natural selection.

5. **How should I live?**

I should live my life morally by being self-reliant, cooperative, nonviolent, and protective of the world's natural resources until I realize I am God.

6. **How do I know what I know?**

I know what I know by reason, logic, and science. I also know what I know by emptying my mind through meditation and contemplation. I also know truth is found in contradiction.

7. **How should I understand our world's history and its future direction?**

I should understand that the world is an illusion, so there is nothing to understand. However, if it isn't an illusion, I am not to understand it because the world is an impersonal, unknowable God.

8. **What should be important to me?**

What should be important to me is recognizing that I am God.

Panentheism

The fifth theological worldview is *panentheism*. Panentheism is also called *Process Theology* or *Finite Godism*. Panentheists believe that "all is *in* god." Developed in the twentieth century primarily by Charles Hartshorne, Alfred North Whitehead, and Schubert Ogden, panentheism mediates between the extreme immanence of pantheism and the extreme transcendence of some theistic models. Panentheists believe that God and the world have a reciprocal relationship. That is, the world needs God in order to exist, and God needs the world to become all that He can be. For the panentheist, God has two poles, a potential pole and a consequential pole. In God's potential pole, God is eternal, unchanging, ideal, and beyond the world. In His consequential pole, God is temporal, changing, real, and identical to the world. In panentheism, values, truth, and morality are grounded in God's nature. However, because God is constantly changing, they are too. Evil exists for the panentheist. However, like man, God is in a state of flux and is constantly striving toward perfection. For this reason, God is not omnipotent and therefore is unable to control evil in the world. The best visual illustration of panentheism is Maxwell Escher's lithograph of hands drawing hands, as Norman Geisler so aptly points out in his book *When Skeptics Ask*. It visually depicts the idea that God is creating the world and the world is creating God. Currently, no major religion subscribes to panentheism. However, some individuals hold to panentheism.

Like Christians, Muslims, deists, atheists, and pantheists, panentheists also vary in their beliefs. For this reason, I will answer their life's most important questions generally.

1. **Who am I?**

   I am a personal, free agent who is a co-creator with God.

2. **What am I?**

   I am only a material body, which houses my intellect, will, and emotions. When I die, I will no longer exist.

3. **Where am I?**

   I am in an uncreated world that depends upon my working together with God for its future.

4. **How did I get here?**

   I got here by evolution and natural selection.

5. **How should I live?**

   I should live my life to help perfect the world and therefore God, since God is not yet perfected in His consequential pole.

6. **How do I know what I know?**

   I know values, truth, and morality are grounded in God's nature. However, since God is constantly changing, they are too. What once was right or moral at one point in history may no longer be right or moral in today's evolving world. I also know what I know through reason, logic, and science.[8]

7. **How should I understand our world's history and its future direction?**

   I should understand that what has happened in the past is the result of a joint effort between God and human beings. The same is true of our future.

8. **What should be important to me?**

   Taking care of the environment and planet earth should be important to me, since God and the world are intertwined. Living in harmony with others as we together work to save our planet should also be important.

Polytheism

The sixth theological worldview is *polytheism*. Polytheists believe in the existence of many finite gods. In polytheism, there is no single god who rules over the entire world. Instead, single gods rule over specific domains of nature. For example, in Hinduism, Parvati is the goddess and daughter of the Himalayas, and Indra is the god of rain and thunder. In polytheism, the gods have a beginning, but no end. They either once were human beings or arose from some aspect of nature. In addition, polytheists believe evil is a necessary part of nature and that the moral laws are given to humans by the gods, who severely punish anyone who breaks them. Hinduism, Buddhism, Confucianism, Taoism, and Shintoism are polytheistic religions.

Since the polytheistic religions vary so much in their beliefs, I will only answer eight of life's most important questions through the eyes of Hinduism because of its increasing popularity in the United States.

1. **Who am I?**

   I am an expression of Brahman and not an individual person who has self-worth.

2. **What am I?**

   I am a material body and an eternal soul (*atman*) that moves from one body to another, suffering the consequences of my past sins committed in past lives. In a past life, I could have been a different person in gender, race, nationality, or socioeconomic status, or even a dog, a cat, or a rat.

3. **Where am I?**

I am in a world that is an illusion (*maya*). The world is only as real as I see it in my mind, and what I see in no way corresponds to what is actually there.

4. **How did I get here?**

I am living out a rebirth (*samsara*) and got in the specific life situation I am in now as a result of the karma I am carrying from my past lives.

5. **How should I live?**

I should live my life by working hard to have good karma so I can one day escape the cycle of rebirths and achieve "eternal bliss" by liberating myself from the bondage of this finite existence (*moksha*).

6. **How do I know what I know?**

I know what I know through the *Vedas, Upanishads, Ramayana, Mahabharata, Bhagavad Gita*, and the *Puranas*, Hinduism's sacred books.

7. **How should I understand our world's history and its future direction?**

I am to understand the world as an extension of *Brahman*, and the material world as being temporary and secondary to people coming to the realization that they too are *Brahman*.

8. **What should be important to me?**

The following should be important to me:

- *Worshiping the gods*
- Worshiping the sacred cow, which has great power
- Understanding salvation is achieved by "the way of works," which is religious duty (*karma marga*); "the way of knowledge," which is understanding man is not a separate entity, but a part of the whole (*jnana marga*); and "the way of devotion," which is public and private worship to a god (*bhakti marga*)
- Obeying Hinduism's virtues and principles (*dharma*)

Henotheism

The seventh theological worldview is *henotheism*. Henotheists are polytheists who believe in many gods. However, this view differs from polytheism in that henotheists only worship one God as preeminent. Mormonism is a henotheistic religion. Since there are 15,082,028 Mormons in the world, I will answer eight of life's most important questions through the eyes of Mormonism.[9]

MORMONISM

1. **Who am I?**

   I am a preexisting, innately good spirit and offspring of God the Father and Mother.

2. **What am I?**

   I am both a material body and preexisting spirit. When I die, my physical body decays, but my preexisting spirit returns from where it came to be with God the Father in the celestial kingdom where I have eternal life as a god if I live as a good Mormon.

3. **Where am I?**

   I am in a universe that once was spirit, but turned into matter. I am also in a place where I am undergoing my test of morality to prove myself worthy of the godhead. Plus, once the world works out its own salvation, just as I am, I am in a place that will one day become the home for "exalted beings."

4. **How did I get here?**

   I got here because I chose wisely in my preexistence to be born on earth and placed into a temporary body so I could undergo the physical temptations and trials of choosing between good and evil to prove myself worthy of being in the godhead. That I chose to come to earth in my preexistence is a testament to the fact that I am a follower of God and not of Lucifer.

5. **How am I supposed to live?**

   I am supposed to live my life in a way that allows me to achieve perfection by learning how to overcome physical temptations while temporarily living in a physical body. This is achieved

169

by being baptized in the Mormon Church, attending church regularly, consistently doing good works, doing temple work, and becoming worthy.

6. **How do I know what I know?**

I know what I know through God the Father, Jesus, and the Holy Ghost (the revelator). All three are ultimate truth, and as such, have revealed truth to me through the *Holy Bible* (as it is translated by the LDS Church),[10] the *Book of Mormon*, the *Doctrines and Covenants,* and the *Pearl of Great Price*. Because truth is grounded in God the Father, Jesus, and the Holy Ghost, truth is absolute and eternal.

7. **How should I understand our world's history and its future direction?**

I am to understand that all of the world's history, as it has been recorded by the secular world, has been twisted, lost, or perverted. However, I know God is in complete control of the universe. I also know His plan of salvation for mankind is through the restored church of Jesus, the Church of Latter-Day Saints.

8. **What should be important to me?**

Being happy should be important to me. In addition, doing everything the Mormon Church tells me to do so I can earn a place in the celestial heaven and live with my family for eternity. Furthermore, I should also tell others God has restored His church—which was lost in a total apostasy—through the Church of Jesus Christ of Latter-Day Saints, so they too can spend their lives working out their salvation and rightful place in heaven.

Dualism

Finally, the last theological worldview is *dualism*. In dualism, reality has two equal poles that are usually viewed as opposites, such as good and evil, matter and spirit, and God and Satan.[11] Zoroastrianism (ancient Iranian religion), Gnosticism (ancient and modern), and the Yin-Yang in Taoism are dualistic religions.

Since these worldviews are not popular in the United States, or well formed, I will not answer eight of life's most important questions from this worldview.

Now let's look at the philosophical worldviews. We are only going to examine two of them. However, they are the two most popular philosophical worldviews in the United States.

Philosophical Worldviews

Naturalism

Naturalism is the belief that the natural world is the only reality there is. Naturalists deny the existence of the supernatural realm and therefore do not believe in God, angels, demons, and immaterial souls. Naturalists exclude all supernatural reasons beforehand (*a priori*) and only look to science for explanations of the universe's wonders. If science hasn't yet discovered something, it doesn't mean some supernatural being like God did it.[12] It simply means science hasn't yet discovered it, but one day will. Some naturalists believe the world popped into existence out of nothing, while others believe it evolved from matter that always existed. For the naturalist, human beings are animals that evolved through the process of evolution and natural selection; morals and values are determined by each person, and therefore are relative and situational; and knowledge and truth are obtained by reason, logic, and science. Naturalists are atheists and answer eight of life's most important questions in much the same way, as you will see.

1. **Who am I?**
   I am an animal that evolved from lower animal forms. I have no eternal value.

2. **What am I?**
   I am only a material body, which houses my intellect, will, and emotions. When I die, I will no longer exist.

3. **Where am I?**
   I am in a closed universe that either popped into existence out of nothing, or organized from uncreated, eternal matter.

4. **How did I get here?**

I got here by chance, random forces, evolution, and natural selection.

5. **How should I live?**

I should live my life to be happy, since my life on earth is the only life I have.

6. **How do I know what I know?**

I know what I know (truth and morality) through reason, logic, and science.

7. **How should I understand our world's history and its future direction?**

I should understand that our world's history and its future direction are determined by man and the natural laws of the universe as discovered by science.

8. **What should be important to me?**

My personal happiness should be important to me.

Postmodernism

Postmodernism is both a historical era as well as a philosophy. In order to understand it as a philosophy, we need to first understand it as a historical era to have the context in which it emerged.

Postmodernism emerged from two historical periods, premodernism and modernism. The premodern era is the time when the human race began up until the time before the seventeenth century. In the premodern era, people looked to God for purpose and meaning in their lives. In premodernity, absolute, objective, universal truth was grounded in God. The second, the modern era, is the seventeenth and eighteenth centuries. In the modern era, people looked to themselves for purpose and meaning in their lives. In modernity, absolute, objective, universal truth was grounded in people, nature, and science.

Today, we live in what is called the *postmodern* era, which began around the mid '80s, early '90s.[13] In postmodernism, people claim there is no way of knowing the purpose and meaning of our lives. They also assert that absolute, objective, and universal truth doesn't exist. Instead, the postmodern philosophy asserts that truth is determined by each person and therefore is relative and situational. For the postmodernist, language is arbitrary and incapable of conveying clear, objective meaning. The same is true of literature.

Therefore, postmodernists believe meaning isn't found in text, but rather emerges from the text as the reader interacts with it. In postmodernism, all comprehensive explanations (metanarratives) developed in the modern era, seeking to make sense of the world, are also rejected. In postmodernism, nothing makes sense. In postmodernism, it's a waste of one's time trying. To the postmodernist, "Christianity is true for you, but not for me"; what you say the Bible teaches is "just your interpretation"; and "all paths lead to God."

Here's how postmodernists answer eight of life's most important questions:

1. **Who am I?**
   I don't know.
2. **What am I?**
   I don't know.
3. **Where am I?**
   I don't know.
4. **How did I get here?**
   I don't know.
5. **How should I live?**
   I don't know.
6. **How do I know what I know?**
   I don't know.
7. **How should I understand our world's history and its future direction?**
   I don't know.
8. **What should be important to me?**
   I don't know.

Now that we know what worldviews are, have examined the ten most common, and have seen how each answers eight of life's most important questions, I want to discuss how Christless worldviews are being passed on to us through the "new oral tradition."

The New Oral Tradition

In the ancient world, worldviews were passed from one generation to the next through speech, songs, folktales, ballads, and chants, otherwise called *the oral tradition*. Today, worldviews are being passed from one generation to the next through television, movies, music, books, art, exercise fads, fashion, and jewelry, or through what I call *the new oral tradition*. Very little in our culture is neutral. Behind every story is a storyteller; every film, a filmmaker; every work of art, an artist; every fashion, a designer; and every piece of jewelry, a silversmith or gold-worker—all who have worldviews, which are being passed on to us through their work.

Irvin Kershner, the director of *The Empire Strikes Back*, said of the movie, "I want to introduce some Zen here."[14] And he did. Kershner popularized Zen Buddhism in America in the '80s when he made Yoda, the little green extraterrestrial, a Zen Master.

George Lucas, the director and producer of *Star Wars*, popularized his view of pantheism in America when he intentionally taught Americans that God was a force.

James Cameron's epic science fiction film, *Avatar*, again popularized pantheism on the big screen in America in the new millennium when a race of blue people called the Na'vi paid homage to Eywa, the "All Mother."

The *New York Times* bestsellers list teen book series and Hollywood blockbuster movies *Percy Jackson & The Olympian: The Lightning Thief* and *Percy Jackson & The Olympian: Sea of Monsters* resurrected ancient Greek polytheism in America among our kids.

The *Harry Potter* series, which grossed $1,328,111,219,[15] and the *Twilight* series, which grossed $3,352,322,180,[16] both written and brought to life on the silver screen, taught our kids spells and incantations along with the belief that witches and vampires can be good as well as evil.

In Hollywood and the Big Apple, the "Evil Eye," a talisman that supposedly wards off evil spirits, is being worn by celebrities such as Lindsay Lohan, Miley Cyrus, Kim Kardashian, and Paris Hilton, and is making its way onto the necks and wrists of unsuspecting women and their daughters, unaware of the conflicting pantheistic worldview it represents, as are Wiccan pentagrams and chakra balancing crystals.

In our gyms, community centers, and churches, yoga, a practice deeply rooted in Hinduism, is practiced today by 20.4 million Americans, 82.2 percent of whom are women,[17] making yoga a 27 billion-dollar industry in America.[18]

These aren't just movies, books, jewelry, and exercises. They are products expressing worldviews that conflict with the traditional Christian worldview. And every time we consume them, wear them, or participate in them, we are letting the people who create them tell us the following:

- How we should and shouldn't view people
- How we should and shouldn't treat people
- What we should and shouldn't tolerate
- How we should and shouldn't use language
- What we should and shouldn't value
- What we should and shouldn't view as good and evil
- What we should and shouldn't believe about truth
- What we should and shouldn't view as moral
- Who we should and shouldn't worship

The Christian's Response

What should we do? Here's what we shouldn't do: We shouldn't follow the two paths Christians typically take when trying to walk the tenuous line of being in the world but not of the world. (1) We shouldn't completely withdraw from the culture and live in a Christian bubble, so we become culturally irrelevant. Not only is doing so unbiblical (our Lord said He was sending His followers out into the world just as His Father had sent Him out into the world [John 17:15–18)] and intentionally interacted with tax collectors [Matt. 9:9–13], prostitutes [Luke 7:36–50], and adulteresses [John 8:1–11] so He could bring God's message of salvation to them), but also it makes unbelievers perceive us as out of touch with reality and hard to relate to. They don't see us as real people living in a real world. Rather they see us as naïve people living in a fantasy world. Also, when unbelievers hear us condemning movies we've never seen, television shows we've never watched, or books we've never read, they don't listen to our opinion, let alone respect what we have to say. Instead, they write us off as intolerant hypocrites who have no clue what we're talking about. And they're right. We don't. (2) We shouldn't immerse ourselves in the culture to the extent that we live no differently from unbelievers. Romans 12:2 tells us not to conform to the pattern of this world, but to be transformed by the renewing of our minds so that we will be able to test and approve what God's good, pleasing, and perfect will is. John, one of the three in Jesus' inner circle, said we are not to be lovers of the world if we are in Christ (1 John 2:15), and Peter, another one, reminds us that we are called out of the darkness and into the light to be "a chosen people," "a royal priesthood," and "a holy nation" (1 Peter 2:9).

So what *should* we do?

If we are to be women who love God with our hearts *and* our minds, we should engage in the culture *where appropriate* and do the following two things:[19] (1) Be cautious of what we consume and critically evaluate everything so that we are able to recognize when worldviews at odds with ours are being passed on to us; (2) use the culture's products as a means by which to share the message of Jesus Christ. What does that look like?

We find out that our friend's teenage daughter has read *Twilight*. So we ask her how she liked it. After we've listened to her tell us what she liked about the book, we tell her what we thought about it because we have actually read it. We may tell her we found the author's view of love interesting, for instance, but very different from God's view of love in the Bible. We compare and contrast both views of love. If we engage our friend's daughter in this way, not only will she respect us, she will probably *listen* to us. And she just might ponder what we said.

If we are to effectively reach people with the message of Jesus Christ, the best way to do it is to enter their world and use what's important to them as a platform for launching spiritual conversations. After all, isn't that what Jesus did?

Discussion Questions

1. What is your worldview?
2. Can you pinpoint influences that specifically shaped it?
3. Would you say your worldview is coherent?
4. If it isn't coherent, what can you do to make it coherent?
5. In our opening stories, which worldview did Alice have? Which worldview did Sophie have?
6. How did their worldviews affect the outcome of their lives? How has your worldview affected the outcome of your life?
7. How do Christianity, Islam, Hinduism, and Mormonism answer eight of life's most important questions similarly and differently?
8. What is the theological implication of the worldviews that hold to the idea that human beings are only made of a material body and not an immaterial soul? Is this a tenable position for Christians to hold? Why or why not?
9. What are the implications of the worldviews that hold to the idea that human beings arose from random chance forces? How does it play into the discussion on abortion, stem cell research, and euthanasia?
10. What movies or television shows have you seen recently that tried to pass a Christless worldview on to you? What about books, art, fashion, or jewelry?
11. Do you agree with the advice to engage in the culture with caution and scrutiny? Why or why not?
12. How could you share the message of Jesus Christ through some of the products of the culture you've evaluated?

Ten

Confession
of a Christless Culture

have a confession to make. I spend lots of money on travel. Why? Because I love to travel. It's one of my favorite things to do. In the past thirteen years, I've been to twenty-seven countries. On my trips, I've traipsed through hundreds, if not thousands, of national landmarks, parks, and historical sites throughout the world. And my journeys aren't limited to overseas. I also enjoy exploring our glorious nation. Fortunately, God gave me a friend who has the same adventurous spirit as I do.

My friend Kathy and I live eighteen miles outside of Washington, D.C. Thirteen years ago, when both of our families moved to northern Virginia from the sweltering state of Arizona, we decided to go into Washington, D.C., once a week, to take in our nation's sights. After I drop off my son at school, we meet up at the West Falls Church Metro Station on the Orange Line of the D.C. Metro and head into the District. Because we arrive an hour before the Smithsonian museums and buildings open, we start our day at our favorite coffee shop. Over a large fat-free mocha with no whip for me, and a medium soy mocha with no whip for her, we catch up on each other's lives. To spectators, it must look like we haven't seen each other in years. The truth is it's only been a week. After that, we go to one of the buildings that make up the Smithsonian and see one exhibit thoroughly before heading back to the suburbs so I can pick up my son from school.

What strikes me every time I go into Washington, D.C., is how many times I see the word *God* inscribed in our nation's federal buildings and national monuments. I see it on the Jefferson and Lincoln Memorials, the National Archives, the Library of Congress, the U.S. Supreme Court, and the Senate and House office buildings. Whenever I do, I always think that if I were a foreigner visiting this country (as I am so often, visiting other countries), I would think God is pretty important to the people of this nation. In fact, I might conclude He is the very foundation of the nation.

America's Foundation

The United States of America was founded upon a Christian philosophical base. Indeed, our nation began when two groups of people wanted to start a new nation in which they could freely worship God and were willing to risk their very lives to do it. I'm talking about the Pilgrims and the Puritans.

Two distinct groups of people, the Pilgrims and the Puritans disapproved of the Roman Catholic Church and believed that the officially established Church of England retained too much of Roman Catholicism's theology and practices. The Pilgrims, called "Separatists," wanted to separate from the Church of England. The Puritans wanted to purify the Church of England by getting it to adopt the Reformed Theology of John Calvin. However, the Church of England didn't want reformation. Nor did it want rogue churches springing up all over England. Therefore, because the Church of England persecuted the two groups, the Pilgrims came to America in 1620 and the Puritans came in 1630 so that they could live out their faith in a biblical community. Just as "the Mosaic Law had regulated Israel's society in Old Testament days," the Pilgrims and the Puritans wanted "the Scripture's authority" to "regulate New England society."[1] And it did. But it did more than that. It laid the foundation for a nation that was about to develop.

As church historian Bruce Shelley puts it, "Puritanism was a tap-root of later evangelical Christianity with its born-again message. In its stress upon a disciplined 'nation under God' and his laws, it contributed significantly to the national character of the American people."[2] Harvard professor, American historian, and the world's leading authority on American Puritanism, Perry Miller, agrees. He says, "Without some understanding of Puritanism . . . there is no understanding of America."[3]

On July 4, 1776, the thirteen colonies making up America declared their independence from Great Britain. In 1789, six years after these colonies won the Revolutionary War, America elected its first president, George Washington. Washington was a humble man of faith who had a deep respect for the Bible. When he was inaugurated on April 30, 1789, in New York City, wearing a dark brown suit with a sword at his side, Washington stood before the American people, respectfully bowed down, and kissed the Bible. Afterward, he told the American people what he believed God's role was in our nation's affairs.

In his inaugural address, Washington said:

> It would be peculiarly improper to omit in this first official act, my fervent supplications to that Almighty Being who rules over the universe, who presides in the councils of nations . . . that his benediction may consecrate to the liberties and happiness of the people of the United States. . . . No people can be bound to acknowledge and adore the invisible hand, which conducts the affairs of men more than the people of the United States. Every step, by which they have advanced to the character of an independent nation, seems to have been distinguished by some token of providential agency.[4]

In other words, Washington believed our nation was built and directed by God Almighty himself, and that no people on this earth *more* than the people of the United States should understand and acknowledge this.

George Washington also understood that the continued success of our nation was dependent upon weaving religion and morality into the fabric of its society and government. After serving a second term, in September of 1796, Washington gave his farewell address to the nation in a six-thousand-word article that was published and distributed across America. In it he said, "Of all the dispositions and habits which lead to political prosperity, religion and morality are indispensable supports. . . . Reason and experience both forbid us to expect that national morality can prevail in exclusion of religious principle."[5] That is, Washington believed our country would ultimately fail as a nation if it *excluded* faith in God and God's morality from its society and government, because he believed the success of our society and nation depended upon it.

Until the late 1950s, the United States of America continued upon the belief that God and Christianity were the foundations of our nation. Thus, traditional biblical values in marriage, family, and gender were instilled in its people through its laws, education, and entertainment. Monogamous marriages were held in high regard. America's laws protected the welfare of the nuclear family. Traditional values were taught in public schools, and living moral lives was important to most.

America's Shift

But a shift occurred in the 1960s. For the first time in America's history, God and America's biblical foundation were no longer honored to the same degree. What happened? The struggle for racial justice and equality erupted in unwarranted violence, leading Americans to question authority, including God's authority. Feminism and gender equality overturned traditional gender roles. Students revolted and protested against the government, its laws, and academic institutions at unprecedented rates, and America was divided due to its involvement in the Vietnam War.

"Make love, not war" became the American motto. In the Swinging Sixties, everything became permissible: Drugs. Sex. Rock 'n' Roll. Bras were burned. Psychedelic drugs were dropped. Free love was made. Counterculture became mainstream, and sticking it to the establishment became a chief virtue. The picture of America painted in the '60s collided with the one painted in its past. In the Age of Aquarius, maintaining personal freedom was all that mattered. To accommodate this new mindset, in 1973, America altered its laws so that abortion, once considered murder in the eyes of the American people, became legalized as a "woman's right to choose." Traditional values in marriage, family, and gender were also challenged and dismissed as sexist, oppressive, and outdated.

In the 1990s, postmodernism set in. Objective, universal truth was put on trial and found guilty of not existing. Language and literature were seen as arbitrary and incapable of conveying clear, objective meaning. Truth and morality became subjective, relative, and unknowable. As did God.

In America today, "Christianity may be true for you, but it's not true for me."

In America today, "all religions lead to God."

In America today, "that's just your interpretation."

In America today, "hookups" are no longer what a service person does to our phone line, but describes casual sexual encounters. Trolls are no longer mythological creatures, but persons who intentionally antagonize others online by posting inflammatory, irrelevant, or offensive comments or other disruptive content. And rainbows no longer refer only to the sign of God's promise, but to "gay rights."[6]

In America today, marriage is no longer only between a man and a woman, but between a man and a man, and a woman and a woman. Families no longer consist only of a mom, a dad, and their children, but blended, nontraditional, single-parent, cross-generational, never married, grandparent parent, and same-sex parent.

In America today, gender is no longer determined by genitalia, but by a decision one makes.

In America today, the concept of personhood is being reevaluated and is increasingly being determined by a person's ability to contribute to society rather than her infinite value as a child of God, created in God's image.

To adapt to all these radical changes, America is redefining itself. Therefore, it has a confession to make.

America's Confession

America's confession is this: America's history is being rewritten to remove the Christian philosophical base upon which America was founded.

I was raised with the conviction that America was a Christian nation. I was educated in a public school. Each morning, I started my day on my feet facing the American flag, which hung in every classroom, with my hand over my heart, as I proudly said the Pledge of Allegiance in unison with my fellow classmates. At school assemblies, I sang "God Bless America." Every December, I sang traditional Christmas carols like "Silent Night," "O Little Town of Bethlehem," and "Away in a Manger" at the public school's annual Christmas pageant. In my classes, it was not uncommon for my teachers to pray for students who were out sick for the day.

Today, public schools are very different. American flags hanging in the classrooms are challenged. The Pledge of Allegiance is no longer said, or if it is, is severely challenged. "God Bless America" is no longer sung, or if it is, is also challenged. Traditional Christmas music is being banned from holiday concerts, and if a teacher prays for a child out sick for the day, she might lose her job.

In addition, in the name of tolerance, our kids are being taught a new truth. A friend of mine obtained her master's degree in education at a local public university in northern Virginia. The first semester, she took a course on how to handle religious, racial, and ethnic differences in the classroom. On the first day of class, her professor handed out a quiz. On the "True and False" section of the quiz was the statement "America was founded upon Christianity." My friend, two decades younger than I, answered "True" because that is what she too had learned as a first-generation American with two Korean parents. When the professor went over the quiz, he told the class the answer was "False." He went on to tell them that America being founded upon Christianity was a lie they've been told. He was there to shed light on the horrific darkness Americans have been taught for the past two hundred thirty-eight years. Thankfully, Dr. Catherine Millard, and others like her, are working hard to shed light on the fact that it is this professor, and others like him, who is telling the lie.

Dr. Catherine Millard, the founder of Christian Heritage Ministries, has a life mission to preserve America's Christian history. Understanding her education is important to understanding her life's work. She holds a bachelor's degree in American studies from George Mason University, a master's degree in education and American literature from George Mason University, a second master's degree in the Old and New Testaments from Capital Bible Seminary, and a doctorate of ministry in Christian education from Luther Rice Seminary. Highly educated in the disciplines of American history, American literature, theology, and both public and Christian education, Dr. Millard is well qualified to examine America's Christian history. How does she do it?

She does this by comparing what is being taught in the history books used in public and Christian schools to the original documents that contain the facts about America's past. For the last twenty-five years, Dr. Millard has spent thousands of hours in this pursuit in the Library of Congress and its rare books room, the Smithsonian Institution, and the National Archives. What she has found is disturbing. Her research has revealed that America's history is being rewritten by stripping our nation's founding fathers of their Christian faith and calling them atheists, agnostics, deists, or worse. Like who? Like the man who crafted the Declaration of Independence, Thomas Jefferson, for instance.

Thomas Jefferson is known today as a deist. This is what I learned from various Christian authors during my journey in coming to faith in Christ. Current history books are calling Thomas Jefferson a deist as well as an atheist and agnostic. Some people have even called him the devil. However, according to Dr. Millard, none of these titles is accurate because they don't reflect Jefferson's original writings or how Jefferson described himself.

The dictionary Thomas Jefferson used was the 1854 edition of *Noah Webster's Dictionary.* In it, a deist is defined as "one who believes in the existence of God, but denies revealed religion; one who professes no form of religion, but follows the light of nature and reason as his only guides in doctrine and practice; a free-thinker."[7] But according to Dr. Millard, this goes against what Thomas Jefferson actually wrote.

She found Jefferson's "Prayer for Peace," which he delivered on March 4, 1805. In it, Jefferson said:

> I shall need, too, the favor of that Being in whose hands we are, who led our forefathers, as Israel of old, from their native land and planted them in a country flowing with all the necessities and comforts of life, who has covered our infancy with His Providence and our riper years with His wisdom and power, and to whose goodness I ask you to join with me in supplications that He will so enlighten the minds of your servants, guide their councils, and prosper their measures, that whatever they do shall result in your good, and shall secure to you the peace, friendship, and approbation of all nations.[8]

She points out that in the prayer, Jefferson compares the American people and their need for God's guidance to God's chosen people, the Israelites, who were written about in the Old Testament. If Jefferson didn't believe in revealed religion, why did he pray to the same God who led Israel, a God of revealed religion (written revelations from God as recorded in the Bible) to also lead our nation's leaders? In addition, deists also believe God *never* intervenes in the world or its events—ever. However, from this prayer, it is clear Thomas Jefferson clearly believed God *does* intervene. Why would Jefferson pray for God's "providence" if he was a deist and didn't believe God intervened in the world's affairs?

Dr. Millard also found a letter written to Dr. Benjamin Rush, dated April 21, 1803. In it, Jefferson wrote:

> My views . . . are the result of a life of inquiry and reflection, and very different from the anti-Christian system imputed to me by those who know nothing of my opinions. To the corruptions of Christianity I am indeed opposed, but not the genuine precepts of Jesus Himself. I am a Christian in the only sense in which He wished anyone to be, sincerely attached to His doctrines in preference to all others.[9]

She points out that in this letter, Jefferson calls himself a Christian outright. But identifying with a world religion goes against what deists believe. Deists do not call themselves Christians. Jefferson then goes on to tell Dr. Rush that he doesn't hold to a corrupted view of Christianity. He only holds to Jesus' genuine teachings.

As Dr. Millard states, the main argument for the consensus that Thomas Jefferson is a deist, however, is based on a book called *The Jefferson Bible*. Perhaps you've heard of it. In both secular and Christian circles, scholars argue that Jefferson snipped the miracles out of the Bible because he was a deist and didn't believe in miracles. Furthermore, many assert Jefferson called "his new Bible" *The Jefferson Bible*. Is that true?

Dr. Millard said, "Most Americans have been sold the widely accepted myth that Thomas Jefferson wrote his own Bible."[10] To determine if this was true, in 1987, Dr. Millard set out to track it down. Did she find it? Not exactly. What she found was a book resembling the infamous *Jefferson Bible* titled *The Life and Morals of Jesus of Nazareth Extracted Textually from the Gospels in Greek, Latin, French, and English*. Dr. Millard said she found the book "in the Smithsonian Institution and I was not only able to scrutinize it but also able to make photocopies of the Title Page and Table of Contents, both written in Jefferson's own handwriting."[11] On its Table of Contents page Jefferson penned, "A Table of Texts from the Evangelists employed in this Narrative and the order of their arrangement."[12]

There are a couple of intriguing additional facts Dr. Millard points out, which are not included when Thomas Jefferson's deism is discussed in contemporary circles. First, there is only one copy of the original (*The Life and Morals of Jesus . . .*) and it was *not* among Jefferson's extensive book collection, comprised of six thousand books, which Jefferson sold to the Library of Congress. Dr. Millard believes its exclusion is significant. Why? Because it implies the document Jefferson wrote was intended for personal use, much like that of a journal, and was never meant to be reproduced and sold. And today, it is a "museum piece in the custody of the Smithsonian Institution" because it is considered to be a personal item of Thomas Jefferson's, not a book to be included in the Library of Congress. Why did he write it? Only Thomas Jefferson knows the real reason, but what he wrote on the Table of Contents page may give us insight into why he wrote it. Apparently, he wanted to document the events surrounding the life, ministry, and death of Jesus and arrange the events in a way that made sense to him so he could study them. But we will never know exactly why he wrote it, or excluded its miracles, because he is not alive for us to ask.

Second, in 1904, when the fifty-seventh Congress ordered 9,000 copies of Jefferson's book to be printed and bound, 3,000 of which were distributed to the Senate, and 6,000 to the House, the name of it was changed to *The Jefferson Bible*—seventy-eight years *after* Thomas Jefferson died. Dr. Millard considers it unfortunate that Jefferson's original title was replaced with *The Jefferson Bible*. He never rewrote the Bible, nor did he ever give permission for the book he *did* write to be renamed as such. He was already dead when it happened.

Three, the book he wrote was altered by removing the Bible chapter and verse references and writing the text as a narrative. Furthermore, none of Jefferson's original commentary or opinions were included.

After comparing the original document Jefferson wrote to the book his deism is based on today, Dr. Millard concludes, "The rewritten version of 1904 is misleading at best, giving the false impression that Thomas Jefferson 'wrote his own Bible.'"[13]

David Barton agrees that Jefferson was most likely not a deist, as he explains in his book *The Jefferson Lies: Exposing the Myths You've Always Believed About Thomas Jefferson*. At the very least, the facts these authors lay out give us good reason to pause and not so readily accept the claims that he "clearly" was a deist. Given the evidence, I don't think it's clear at all.

Implications

The question we have to ask ourselves is why would anyone strip Thomas Jefferson, or any of the other founding fathers of this nation, of their Christian faith?

The reason is this: If the founding fathers are stripped of their Christian faith, they did not build America upon a Christian philosophical base. This means Christianity no longer has any special right to be accepted in the public arena any more than does Islam or any other religion or philosophy. And this is exactly what we are beginning to see.

At Sonora State University in California, a practicing Catholic student was asked to remove her cross necklace twice when she worked at a freshman orientation because her cross might "offend" non-Christian students.[14] A pastor from North Carolina was fired from his job as an honorary chaplain for the state House of Representatives for invoking the name of Jesus at the end of a prayer.[15] In a retirement home in Port Wentworth, Georgia, the residents were told they were no longer allowed to pray before meals.[16] An eight-year-old boy in Massachusetts was forced to leave school and have a psychiatric evaluation for drawing a picture of Jesus on a cross.[17] A University of Kentucky professor didn't get a job directing the university's observatory because the committee doing the hiring found out he was a Christian.[18] A public schoolteacher in New York had to remove all inspirational wall hangings and plaques with Bible verses on them along with a quote by one of America's former presidents, Ronald Reagan, which said, "If we forget that we are one nation under God, then we will be a nation gone under."[19] An older woman in Minnesota who lives in low-income housing was told she couldn't read her Bible, pray, or speak about her faith with her friends who came to visit her when she was with them in the commons area of the apartment complex in which she lived.[20] A man in Phoenix hosted a Bible study in his home and was given a sixty-day jail sentence because he was told it violated city zoning laws.[21] A "U.S. military training brief labeled Catholics and evangelical Christians as religious extremists."[22] The IRS unfairly targeted Christian ministries and pro-life groups for extensive audits along with other conservative, right-leaning groups, one of which was The Billy Graham Evangelistic Association.[23]

However, the University of Michigan-Dearborn spent $25,000 in taxpayer dollars installing footbaths in its bathrooms for its Muslim students, which only make up 10 percent of its student body.[24] Judicial Watch, an organization committed to ensuring that the American government does not abuse its power, caught the FBI purging all its anti-terrorism training documents of any material that might be "offensive" to Muslims.[25] In a Colorado public high school, all students were led in the Arabic translation of the Pledge of Allegiance to include "one nation under Allah."[26] A Texas public school geography teacher encouraged American students to wear Islamic clothing and to think of the men who flew American jetliners into the Pentagon and the World Trade Centers on 9/11 not as terrorists, but "freedom fighters."[27] In Indiana, kids attending a public school "were forced" to sing a song declaring that "Allah was God" in a holiday concert.[28] And an attorney in Tennessee warned American citizens that if they dared to criticize a Muslim on social networking sites such as Facebook or Instagram, they could be found guilty of violating "federal civil rights."[29] President Barack Obama said the celebration of Ramadan "reminds us that Islam is part of the fabric of our nation."[30] He also said "that Islam has contributed to the character of our country and Muslim Americans, and their good works, have helped to *build* our nation."[31]

Make no mistake. There is a movement from within America to rewrite the Christian philosophical base out of our nation's history. And that is not all. God is being erased with it. Last year, when America celebrated the 150-year anniversary of Abraham Lincoln's Gettysburg Address, President Barack Obama recited it from the Soldiers' National Cemetery in Gettysburg, Pennsylvania, in a televised program for the listening world to hear. In the original address, Lincoln's words were "that this nation, under God, shall have a new birth of freedom." However, when our Commander in Chief publicly recited it, he modified it, saying, "that this nation shall have a new birth of freedom" omitting Lincoln's *actual* words that included "*under God.*"[32]

I wonder how many people who heard the Gettysburg Address for the first time from Barack Obama think Abraham Lincoln was an atheist because he didn't mention God in it. And will the onlooking world, and America's younger generations, also believe that God was never important to the founders of this nation as American presidents, and other important governmental officials, textbooks, and public schoolteachers, continue to remove His name from the founding fathers' documents, prayers, and speeches? I'll let you be the judge. It's only a matter of time before the phrase "In God We Trust" is removed from American currency, which made its first entrance into America on a two-cent coin in 1864, when Congress passed an Act on April 22. Who knows? Maybe one day it will say, "In Allah We Trust."

Does any of this surprise you? It shouldn't. Jesus warned Christians they would be persecuted for His name's sake (John 15:21) and that this persecution would accelerate in the "last days" (Rev. 13:10).

Todd Starnes says in his eye-opening book *God Less America: Real Stories From the Front Lines of the Attack on Traditional Values*, that Pastor Rick Warren told him religious freedom is the "civil rights issue of our generation."[33] Starnes says, given that "public schools are indoctrinating our children with the gospel of secularism, Hollywood is spewing toxins into our homes, the American family is in ruins," and "what was once wrong is now right and what was once right is now wrong," he agrees.[34]

There is an attack on Christianity in America, and the outbreak is spreading like a malignant, incurable cancer. As it continues to metastasize, persecution of Christians in America is ramping up to stage four. If the war on Christianity in this nation continues at this pace, and at the insidious level it is, it might not be long before Christianity is illegal in America.

If we are to be women who love God with our hearts *and* our minds, it's vital that we prepare ourselves, and our kids, to emotionally, intellectually, and spiritually cope with living as Christians in an increasingly Christless culture.

Discussion Questions

1. What were you taught about America's foundation when you were growing up?

2. Have you encountered the word *God* or Christian Scriptures inscribed in government or public buildings in the United States outside of Washington, D.C.? If so, where? What were the inscriptions? Are there already attempts to have them removed?

3. Did you learn Thomas Jefferson was a deist? If so, what evidence was the claim based upon?

4. Which other founding fathers have you heard were atheists, agnostics, and deists? Do the claims have merit?

5. Can you cite other specific examples of Christians being unfairly treated in this country, while people of other faiths are being given special treatment?

6. How does knowing there is a movement within America to rewrite our history by eliminating God and Christianity as a formative influence affect how you interact with the culture today?

7. Do you think the prediction that Christianity might one day be illegal in America has merit? If so, why?

Conclusion

A month ago, I decided to take figure-skating lessons. This idea wasn't the result of a midlife crisis. Rather, it was the result of a friend challenging another friend to pursue a dream. My friend Irina has been taking figure-skating lessons for the past five years. Over the years, she has often talked to me about the joy figure skating brings her. Whenever she talked about it, my ears perked up, because learning to figure skate is something I've always wanted to do. Sensing this, Irina invited to me join her sometime. I eventually decided to take her up on her offer and went with her several times. Every time I went with her, Irina taught me some basic skills. Because some of the skills came easily for me, Irina encouraged me to take a few lessons. I agreed to try it and had my first lesson a little over a month ago. I really enjoyed it. In fact, I liked it so much that I wanted to begin practicing what I learned the very next day. When I was practicing, I exercised caution because I didn't want to hurt myself. For instance, when I worked on skills at which I felt particularly shaky, I practiced them off the ice until I felt more comfortable doing them on the ice to avoid hurting myself. After practicing for an hour, I went to get a drink of water. Then it happened.

When I got back onto the ice, I heard raucous behavior directly behind me. I looked to see what was going on, and I saw a group of teenage boys flailing their arms and kicking their legs, coming straight at me. It looked like they were going to knock me over like a bowling ball taking down its last pin. While the events that unfolded next are still blurry, what I do know is that it felt like someone grabbed my feet, lifted them up and off the ice, gave my body a half-twist, and threw me down, hard, on my left shoulder. It really hurt when it happened, but I was too angry and embarrassed to let anyone know it did. Allowing my pride to get the best of me, I quickly got up, refusing the hand of one of the boys who offered to help me.

After assuring the group of boys that I was indeed all right in the wake of their shenanigans, I quickly skated over to the other side of the rink to get as far away from them as I could. If I was to continue practicing, I knew I needed to mentally, emotionally, and physically shake it off. I was certain any physical pain that remained would pass, along with my bruised ego. I wasn't going to let one dreadful fall prevent me from finishing practice. Except when I started practicing again, the physical pain was still there. In fact, it was getting worse. Unfortunately, it wasn't until I realized I couldn't lift my left arm more than a few inches that I thought I should probably get off the ice, go home, and put ice on it.

It turns out I fractured the greater tuberosity (part of the upper humerus bone) and damaged my rotator cuff. I am still in quite a bit of pain today. Truth be told, it still really hurts to lift up my left arm. But lift it up I must, because I am told that if I don't, my shoulder could lock. If that happens, I will really be in trouble. Apparently, to prevent broken shoulders from locking, they aren't put in casts or slings, but instead must be given range-of-motion exercises daily regardless of how painful it is so that full range of motion isn't lost. So that is what I must do.

When I reflect back to the day of the incident and how I've handled living with the pain, I've noticed something interesting. When I fell, my first instinct was to ignore the pain. I thought that if I pretended the pain wasn't there, it didn't exist. But when that didn't work, I thought that if I just rested my shoulder for a couple of days, the pain would go away on its own. But when that didn't work, I thought that if I just popped a pain pill every four to six hours for a few days, the pain would go away. But when that didn't work either, I thought that if I just exercised my shoulder with my personal trainer, Kota, once a week for a couple of weeks, the pain would go away. But when that didn't work, I finally remembered something I've learned in the fifty years I've walked this earth, but had temporarily forgotten in the midst of my pain. It is this: The only way to achieve success in anything, including overcoming physical, emotional, psychological, or spiritual challenges, is by taking full responsibility for them and then doing the hard work required to either achieve them or recover from them. And when it comes to strengthening a weakness, there is no quick fix. There is no magic pill. There is no easy way.

King David once said that "even though" he walked "through the darkest valley," he would "fear no evil" because he was certain God was with him and would comfort him (Psalm 23:4). He didn't expect God to instantly take away the bad circumstances in which he found himself. Instead, he *accepted* that he had to walk through the difficult circumstances he was in and fully trust God to help him through it. Reflecting on King David's words made me remember that the only way I was ever going to get *over* the pain I was in was to go *through* the pain. This meant I couldn't ignore it or somehow try to escape it. Instead, I had to face it. Feel it. Accept it. It also meant I had to take full responsibility for it and be an active participant in my shoulder's recovery. After recalling this lesson, I finally made the decision to actually *do* the exercises that my orthopedic surgeon, physical therapist, and trainer gave me, exercises I had previously ignored. I also decided to do them consistently, every day, no matter how much doing them hurt.

I've been doing the exercises for a little over a week now. Doing them is extremely painful. Sometimes they are so painful I want to quit. But I don't. I press on, because I'm learning that when I do them consistently, every day, the pain is a little less severe the next day. I'm also noticing that my shoulder is finally starting to get better. Yes, the progress is slow. And yes, I still have a long way to go. And yes, I am still in a tremendous amount of pain. However, I'm finding that when I give my shoulder the environment it needs (daily range-of-motion exercises, ice, and the gift of time), it is finally starting to heal. I am confident that if I am patient, do the hard work necessary to overcome the damage done to my shoulder, persevere through the pain, and realize that recovery is a process, my shoulder will heal—eventually.

Loving God with our hearts *and* our minds involves the same treatment if we are to have a healthy and balanced faith. First, we need to recognize that the only way we are ever going to achieve success engaging our minds in our faith in addition to our hearts is by taking responsibility for our faith, including the weak areas. Once we've done that, we need to do the hard work of incorporating apologetics into our lives as a daily spiritual discipline, along with Bible study and prayer, to continue strengthening any weaknesses.

Our first instinct may be to ignore our weaknesses and pretend that we don't have any areas that need strengthening. We may also want to believe that some of our under-formulated beliefs will somehow become better formulated and strengthened all by themselves, on their own. We may even want to believe that God will miraculously zap us with a stronger belief system that we are able to defend well if we just consistently pray for it long enough. We may even want to believe that it is our pastor's job, or the director of women's ministries' job, to help us strengthen the weak areas. But if we are honest with ourselves, we know deep down that these fantasies won't become realities.

If we are to be women who love God with our hearts *and* our minds, so that our faith is balanced and strong, we must first accept that strengthening the weak areas of our faith is our responsibility and no one else's. Next, we must resolve to become active participants in our faith by being willing to use the tool God gave us—apologetics. After that, we must recognize that the only way to get *over* the weak areas of our faith is by working *through* the weak areas of our faith. There is no other way. There is no easy way. Finally, we must make a commitment to ourselves (and others if necessary) that we will work on the weak areas of our faith consistently, every day, no matter how hard it is.

At times, we might want to quit. But we must not. We must press on, because when we do, we will discover that as we strengthen our weaknesses and get better at defending our faith, it will feel a little less painful with each passing day. Yes, our progress may feel slow. And yes, we might have a long way to go. And yes, it might feel downright painful at times. However, I am confident that when we give the weak areas of our faith the environment they need (a small dose of apologetics incorporated into our lives on a daily basis as a spiritual discipline along with Bible study, prayer, and the gift of time), the weak areas of our faith will strengthen—eventually!

The Christian faith isn't for the faint of heart. It's a faith that requires that we engage more than our hearts. It's a faith that requires that we love God with our minds in addition to our hearts, because this is the kind of faith Jesus calls His believers to have (Matt. 22:37). As you go forward, I challenge you to continue reading more books like this one. I also challenge you to attend apologetics classes, seminars, and conferences. I am confident that the more you continue to love God with your heart *and* your mind, the more confident you will be that Christianity is an intellectually defensible faith. And the more confident you will be that your faith can handle any type of scrutiny that comes your way. And when it does, I am positive you will discover that because you know what you believe and are able to defend those beliefs well, you will no longer be afraid to share your faith with anyone who will listen. And if people lash out at you and/or call you names when you're having spiritual conversations with them, you will no longer take it as a personal attack, as you once did (if you did), because you will see the attack for what it is—a tactic used to deflect your attention away from the real issues being discussed: the truth-claims of Christianity.

When you continue to love God with your heart *and* your mind, not only will you discover that the weak areas of your faith are strengthened but also that your mind and your heart are brought into harmony as well. And perhaps for the first time in your life, your faith will feel integrated, authentic, and whole. And you will feel integrated, authentic, and whole because of it. I am convinced, my dear sister in Christ, that as you continue to love God with your heart *and* your mind, your faith will transform from ordinary to extraordinary!

Notes

Chapter 2: You Are What You Believe

1. Edward W. Goodrick and John R. Kohlenberger, III, *The Strongest NIV Exhaustive Concordance* (Grand Rapids, MI: Zondervan, 1999), 128.

2. Ibid., 1187.

3. William T. Ellis, *Billy Sunday, the Man and His Message: With His Own Words, Which Have Won Thousands for Christ* (Philadelphia: Universal Book and Bible House, 1914), 77.

4. Tom Morris, *Philosophy for Dummies* (New York: Wiley Publishing, Inc., 1999), 41.

5. Goodrick and Kohlenberger, *The Strongest NIV Exhaustive Concordance*, 1179.

6. Emphasis mine.

7. Emphasis mine.

8. Emphasis mine.

9. John C. Maxwell, *Today Matters: 12 Daily Practices to Guarantee Tomorrow's Success* (New York: Center Street, 2004), 53.

10. Ibid.

Chapter 3: Thinking Well Becomes Her

1. James B. Nance and Douglas J. Wilson, *Intermediate Logic for Christian and Home Schools* (Moscow, ID: Canon Press, 1990), 1.

2. Ibid.

3. Albert Einstein as cited in John Maxwell, *How Successful People Think* (New York: Center Street, 2009), xi.

Chapter 4: A Bad Thought Day

1. Einstein and Maxwell, *How Successful People Think*.

2. James B. Nance and Douglas J. Wilson, *Introductory Logic for Christian and Home Schools* (Moscow, ID: Canon Press, 2006), 223.

3. Ibid., 217.

4. Ibid., 219.

5. Christopher Hitchens, *God Is Not Great: How Religion Poisons Everything* (New York: Hachette Book Group, 2007), 64.

6. Abraham Lincoln as cited in Deborah J. Bennett, *Logic Made Easy: How to Know When Language Deceives You* (New York: W. W. Norton & Company, 2004), 40.

Chapter 5: Heaven's Bestseller

1. Hos. 1:1; Joel 1:1; Mic. 1:1; Zeph. 1:1; cf. Jonah 1:1; Hag. 1:1; Zech. 1:1.

2. Acts 8:14; 11:1; 12:24; 13:7, 44; 15:35; 1 Thess. 2:13.

3. Rom. 3:1–2; Matt. 1:22; 4:4; 15:4; 22:31–32; Mark 7:9–13; Acts 3:18; Acts 7:38; and Heb. 1:1.

4. Matt. 22:43; Acts 1:16; 4:25; 28:25; Heb. 3:7; 10:15; 2 Peter 1:20–21.

5. 1 Tim. 5:18, cf. Luke 10:7; 2 Peter 3:16, cf. Paul's letters.

6. Norman Geisler and William Nix, *A General Introduction to the Bible* (Chicago: Moody Press, 1968, 1986), 34.

7. Emphasis mine.

8. Paul Little, *Know What You Believe: A Practical Discussion of the Fundamentals of the Christian Faith* (Colorado Springs, Cook, 1970), 14.

9. Brad Harrub, PhD, "Evolution Frauds," 2005, https://evolutionisntscience.wordpress.com/evolution-frauds/ (accessed February 6, 2015).

10. Jeff Miller, PhD, "Cro-Magnon: Man Nothing but a 'Modern' Man," http://www.apologeticspress.org/APContent.aspx?category=9&article=3501 (accessed Feb. 4, 2015).

11. Ibid.

12. Biologos.com, "How are the ages of the Earth and universe calculated?" Last modified April 16, 2012, http://biologos.org/questions/ages-of-the-earth-and-universe (accessed December 24, 2014).

13. Ken Ham, *The New Answers Book 1: Over 25 Questions on Creation/Evolution and the Bible* (Green Forest, AR: Master Books, 2006), 117–118.

Chapter 6: The Real Deal

1. Hank Hanegraaff, "M-A-P-S to Guide You through Biblical Reliability." DB011, 1.

2. Merriam-Webster Dictionary, "extant," http://www.merriam-webster.com/dictionary/extant (accessed December 26, 2014).

3. Josh McDowell, *Evidence That Demands a Verdict: Historical Evidence for the Christian Faith,* vol. 1 (Nashville: Thomas Nelson, 1972), 40.

4. Ibid., 42–43.

5. Ken Samples, *A World of Difference: Putting Christian Truth-Claims to the Worldview Test* (Grand Rapids, MI: Baker Books, 2007), 93.

6. Ibid., 94.

7. McDowell, *Evidence That Demands a Verdict,* 42.

8. Geisler and Nix, *A General Introduction to the Bible,* 468.

9. Ibid.

10. McDowell, *Evidence That Demands a Verdict,* 43.

11. Ibid.

12. McDowell, *Evidence That Demands a Verdict*, 52.

13. Ibid., 50.

14. Aaron Allen, "The Authenticity and Reliability of the Bible," Lecture at Trinity Christian School, Fairfax, VA, September 7, 2012.

15. Hanegraaff, "M-A-P-S to Guide You through Biblical Reliability," 2.

16. Craig Blomberg as cited in Lee Strobel, *The Case for Christ: A Journalist's Personal Investigation of the Evidence for Jesus* (Grand Rapids, MI: Zondervan, 1998), 50.

17. McDowell, *Evidence That Demands a Verdict*, 73.

18. John McRay, *Archaeology and The New Testament* (Grand Rapids, MI: Baker Academic, 1991), 188–189.

19. Ibid., 203–204.

20. Christianitytoday.com, Ben Witherton, III, September 1, 2003, "Top Ten New Testament Archeological Finds of the Past 150 Years," http://www.christianity today.com/ct/2003/septemberweb-only/9–22–21.0.html?start=3 (accessed January 13, 2015).

21. Ibid.

22. McRay, *Archaeology and the New Testament*, 204.

23. Ibid., 206–210.

24. Ibid., 217–221.

25. McRay, *Archeology and the New Testament*, 154.

26. McDowell, *Evidence That Demands a Verdict*, 71.

27. Ibid., 70–71.

28. Hanegraaff, "M-A-P-S to Guide You through Biblical Reliability," 2.

29. McDowell, *Evidence That Demands a Verdict*, 141.

30. Ibid., 175.

31. Ibid., 144–166.

32. Geisler and Nix, *A General Introduction to the Bible*, 360.

33. Ibid.

34. Allaboutarcheology.org, "Dead Sea Scrolls, Part I," http://www.allabout archaeology.org/dead-sea-scrolls-2.htm (accessed January 9, 2015).

35. Gleason Archer as cited in Geisler and Nix, *A General Introduction to the Bible*, 367.

36. Hanegraaff, "M-A-P-S to Guide You through Biblical Reliability," 3.

37. Peter Stone as cited in McDowell, *Evidence That Demands a Verdict*, 167.

38. Ibid.

39. Ibid.

40. Ibid.

41. McDowell, *Evidence That Demands a Verdict*, 73.

Chapter 7: Got Issues?

1. Geisler and Nix, *A General Introduction to the Bible*, 235.

2. Ibid., 218.

3. Geisler and Nix, *A General Introduction to the Bible*.

4. The Interlinear Bible is not technically a translation, but rather is the original Hebrew, Greek, and Aramaic text. However, the original languages are keyed

through *Strong's Concordance* using the KJV or the NAS, so that we know what the original text says. The Interlinear Bible is the best literal translation available and is what many Bible scholars use.

Chapter 8: The Rolling Stone

1. Gary Habermas and Michael R. Licona, *The Case for the Resurrection of Jesus* (Grand Rapids, MI: Kregel, 2004), 26.
2. Ibid., 44.
3. Ibid., 75.
4. Flavius Josephus, *The Complete Works of Josephus: Antiquities* 18.64, William Whiston, trans. (Grand Rapids, MI: Kregel, 1999), 590.
5. Habermas and Licona, *The Case for the Resurrection of Jesus*, 49.
6. Ibid.
7. Ibid., 50. Mara Bar-Serapion was an Assyrian Stoic philosopher who wrote about Jesus in AD 73.
8. William D. Edwards, Wesley J. Gabel, and Floyd E. Hosmer, "On the Death of Jesus Christ," March 21, 1986.
9. John Dominic Crossan, *Jesus: A Revolutionary Biography* (San Francisco: Harper Collins, 1994), 145; cf. 154, 196, 201 as cited by Gary Habermas, *The Risen Jesus & Future Hope* (New York: Rowman & Littlefield, 2003), 17.
10. Ibid., 153.
11. Peter was crucified upside down. Andrew was crucified. James was beheaded. Matthew was speared to death. Bartholomew was beaten and then crucified. Philip was crucified. Thomas was speared to death. Simon the Zealot was crucified. James was stoned to death. Thaddaeus was stoned to death, and Paul was beheaded.
12. Habermas and Licona, *The Case for the Resurrection of Jesus*, 59–60.
13. Gary R. Habermas, *The Risen Jesus and Future Hope* (Oxford: Littlefield Publishers, 2003), 28.
14. Habermas and Licona, *The Case for the Resurrection of Jesus*, 69.
15. Ibid.
16. Ibid., 69–70.
17. Ibid., 74.
18. Ibid., 76.
19. *Famous Quotes by Christian Leaders,* "The Resurrection of the Lord Jesus Christ," http://www.geocities.com/cobblestoneministries/2005_CRM/TheResurrection_QuotesbyChristianLeaders (accessed November 18, 2008).

Chapter 9: Through the Looking Glass

1. Patrick J. Hurley, *A Concise Introduction to Logic*, 8th ed. (Belmont, WA: Wadsworth, 2003), 173.
2. Gen. 1:26–27; John 1:12.
3. Ps. 139:14; Matt. 6:26.
4. Matt. 10:28.
5. Simon Hooper, "The Rise of the 'New Atheists,'" Cnn.com, Nov. 9, 2006, http://www.cnn.com/2006/WORLD/europe/11/08/atheism.feature/index.html?iref=allsearch (accessed September 30, 2014).

6. For additional information on discussing the existence of God, see Appendix B: "Hello, Is Anyone There?"

7. The immanence of pantheism is different from the immanence of theism in that pantheists believe God is actually a part of the universe in His very being. Theists believe God permeates the universe, but is not physically a part of it, since God is spirit only.

8. Brian McLaren also gleans truth from a very liberal interpretation of the Bible.

9. Mormonnewsroom.com, "Facts and Statistics," last modified March 18, 2014, http://www.mormonnewsroom.org/facts-and-statistics (accessed October 14, 2014).

10. Joseph Smith edited, revised, added to, and deleted from the King James Version of the Bible, making a new KJV Bible the Mormon Church calls the "Inspired Version."

11. It is important for the Christian to recognize that this worldview makes God and Satan equals. They are not. God is infinitely more powerful than Satan, as Satan is one of God's fallen creations and under the sovereignty of God.

12. This idea is called the "God of the gaps." Naturalists accuse Christians of appealing to the "God of the gaps" when science can't explain something. It's the idea that since science can't figure something out, God must have done it, and therefore fills in the gaps.

13. Some philosophers assert that the culture in which we live is no longer postmodern. However, they are unclear as to what type of historical era we have progressed.

14. Geisler and Brooks, *When Skeptics Ask*, 42.

15. The-numbers.com, "Box Office Numbers for Harry Potter Movies," http://www.the-numbers.com/movies/franchise/Harry-Potter (accessed October 23, 2014).

16. The-numbers.com, "Box Office Numbers for Twilight Movies," http://www.the-numbers.com/movies/franchise/Twilight (accessed October 23, 2014).

17. The Huffington Post, "American Yoga: How Many People Practice It in the United States," December 7, 2012, http://www.huffingtonpost.com/2012/12/06/american-yoga_n_2251360.html (accessed October 23, 2014).

18. The Huffington Post, "How Yoga Became a $27 Billion Industry—and Reinvented American Spirituality," December 16, 2014, http://www.huffingtonpost.com/2013/12/16/how-the-yoga-industry-los_n_4441767.html (accessed October 23, 2014).

19. Notice I said "where appropriate." I am not suggesting Christians watch R-rated movies, read books with questionable moral values, or view crude television shows. There is a lot in the culture that does not involve profanity, nudity, or explicit sex. What I am suggesting is that Christians engage in the culture under the guidance of the Holy Spirit to determine what is, and isn't, appropriate for them.

Chapter 10: Confession of a Christless Culture

1. Ken Curtis, "Who Were the Puritans?" Christianity.com, www.Christianity.com/church/church-history/timeline/1601–1700/who-were-the-puritans-11630087.html (accessed October 1, 2014).

2. Shelley, *Church History in Plain Language*, 292.

3. Perry Miller, as cited in James P. Stobaugh, *American History: Observations and Assessments from Early Settlement to Today* (Green Forest, AR: Master Books, 2012), 40.

4. Ralph K. Andrist, *George Washington: A Biography in His Own Words* (New York: Harper & Row, 1972), 174, as cited in Sims and Gore, *George Washington: A Timeless Hero*, 87.

5. Ibid., 98.

6. Todd Starnes, *God Less America: Real Stories From the Front Lines of the Attack on Traditional Values* (Lake Mary, FL: Frontlines Publishing, 2014), 1.

7. As cited in Catherine Millard, *The Rewriting of America's History* (Camp Hill, PA: Christian Publications, Inc., 1991), 91.

8. Ibid., 91–92.

9. Ibid., 92.

10. Millard, *The Rewriting of America's History*, 97.

11. Ibid.

12. Ibid.

13. Ibid., 99.

14. Eric Owens, "Student ordered to remove cross necklace at California college," dailycaller.com, http://dailycaller.com/2013/07/03/student-ordered-to -remove-cross-necklace-at-sonoma-state-university, 3 July 2013 (accessed October 4, 2014).

15. Mark Becker, "CMPD chaplains told to stop invoking Jesus at public events," WSOCTV, June 19, 2012, http://www.wsoctv.com/news/news/local/cmpd-chap lains-told-stop-invoking-jesus-public-eve/nPZdq/ (accessed October 12, 2014).

16. First Amendment Center, "Meal Prayer at Georgia Senior Center Stopped, Then Restored," May 11, 2010, http://www.firstamendmentcenter.org/meal-prayer -at-ga-senior-center-stopped-then-restored (accessed October 12, 2014).

17. Gerry Tuoti, "Taunton Second-Grader Sent Home Over Drawing of Jesus," *Taunton Daily Gazette*, December 15, 2009, http://www.tauntongazette.com /x1903566059/Taunton-second-grader-suspended-over-drawing-of-Jesus as cited in Starnes, *God Less America: Real Stories From the Front Lines of the Attack on Traditional Values*, 9.

18. Mark Oppenheimer, "Astronomer Sues the University of Kentucky, Claiming His Faith Cost Him a Job," December 18, 2010, http://www.nytimes.com /2010/12/19/us/19kentucky.html (accessed October 14, 2014).

19. American Freedom Law Center, "Christian Teacher Sues New York Public School District for Restricting Her Religious Speech," January 10, 2013, http://www .americanfreedomlawcenter.org/press-release/christian-teacher-sues-new-york-pub lic-school-district-for-restricting-her-religious-speech/ (accessed October 14, 2014).

20. Alliance Defending Freedom, "Evicting a Widow's Prayer," October 19, 2012, http://alliancedefendingfreedom.org/News/PRDetail/7706 (accessed October 14, 2014).

21. The Rutherford Institute, "Arizona Man Jailed for 60 Days for Home Bible Study to Appear in Court for Violating Probation by Holding Additional Bible Studies on His Property," July 16, 2012, https://www.rutherford.org/publications _resources/on_the_front_lines_/ariz_man_jailed_for_60_days_for_home_bible _study_to_appear_in_court_for_vio (accessed October 14, 2014).

22. Lachan Markay, "Defense Department Classifies Catholics, Evangelicals as Extremists," *Washington Times*, April 5, 2013, http://www.washingtontimes .com/news/2013/apr/5/dod-presentation-classifies-catholics-evangelicals/?page=1 as cited in Todd Starnes, *God Less America: Real Stories From the Front Lines of the Attack on Traditional Values* (Lake Mary: Charisma Media/Charisma House Book Group, 2014), 7.

23. Starnes, *God Less America,* 7–8.

24. Tamar Lewin, "Some U.S. Universities Install Foot Baths for Muslim Students," *New York Times,* August 7, 2007, http://nytimes.com/2007/08/07/world /americas/07iht-muslisms.4.7022566.html (accessed October 4, 2014).

25. Judicial Watch, JW Report: "U.S. Government Purges of Law Enforcement Training Material Deemed 'Offensive' to Muslims," December 9, 2013, http:// www.tinyurl.com/lhvqn3r (accessed October 13, 2014).

26. Nick McGurk, "Fort Collins Students Read Pledge of Allegiance in Arabic," 9News.com, January 29, 2013, http://www.9news.com/rss/article/313505/188 /Students-read-pledge-in-Arabic (October 14, 2014).

27. Todd Starnes, "Students Told to Call 9/11 Hijackers 'Freedom Fighters,'" Fox News Radio, http://radio.foxnews.com/toddstarnes/top-stories/students-told -to-call-9-11-hijackers-freedom-fighters.html (accessed October 14, 2014).

28. Starnes, *God Less America,* 164.

29. Ibid., 163.

30. Ibid., 161–162.

31. Ibid., 162. Emphasis mine.

32. Cheryl K. Chumley, "Obama's 'under God' omission in Gettysburg Address sparks fire," *Washington Times*, November 20, 2013, http://www.washingtontimes .com/new/2013/nov/20/obama-under-god-omission-gettysburg-address-sparks (accessed October 2, 2014). Emphasis mine.

33. Starnes, *God Less America,* 3.

34. Ibid.

Appendix A: Belief Inventory Checklist

1. Inventory breakdown based on Kevin Lewis' breakdown of dogmatic and systematic theology. See Kevin Alan Lewis, "Principia and Prolegomena" (class notes for Essential Christian Doctrines, Biola University, 2009), 6–9.

2. Such as God's creation of the spiritual and physical world, miracles, etc.

Appendix B: Hello, Is Anyone There?

1. George Barna Group, "2015 State of Atheism in America," Barna.org, https:// www.barna.org/barna-update/culture/713-2015-state-of-atheism-in-america#.VS PlU7mUBD8 (accessed April 7, 2015).

2. Ibid.

3. J. P. Moreland and William Lane Craig, *Philosophical Foundations for a Christian Worldview* (Downers Grove, IL: InterVarsity Press Academic, 2003), 477.

Appendix A

Belief Inventory Checklist[1]

	I Know What I Believe	I Can Defend This	I Own This Belief
The Bible			
Revelation	☐	☐	☐
Inspiration	☐	☐	☐
Illumination	☐	☐	☐
Authority	☐	☐	☐
Inerrancy	☐	☐	☐
Canonicity	☐	☐	☐
Transmission	☐	☐	☐
Translation	☐	☐	☐
God			
Existence	☐	☐	☐
Knowability	☐	☐	☐
Deficient Views	☐	☐	☐
Names	☐	☐	☐
Essence & Attributes	☐	☐	☐
Triunity	☐	☐	☐
Sovereignty	☐	☐	☐
Works[2]	☐	☐	☐

Belief Inventory Checklist

	I Know What I Believe	I Can Defend This	I Own This Belief
Jesus Christ			
Deity	☐	☐	☐
Humanity	☐	☐	☐
Incarnation	☐	☐	☐
Suffering	☐	☐	☐
Death & Burial	☐	☐	☐
Descent Into Hell	☐	☐	☐
Resurrection	☐	☐	☐
Ascension	☐	☐	☐
Apocalypse	☐	☐	☐
Atonement	☐	☐	☐
Offices of Prophet, Priest, and King	☐	☐	☐
Holy Spirit			
Person	☐	☐	☐
Works	☐	☐	☐
Man			
Creation	☐	☐	☐
Makeup	☐	☐	☐
Origin of Soul	☐	☐	☐
God's Image Bearer	☐	☐	☐
Sin			
Origin	☐	☐	☐
Essence	☐	☐	☐
Transmission	☐	☐	☐
Original Sin	☐	☐	☐
Actual Sin	☐	☐	☐
Salvation			
Grace	☐	☐	☐
Election	☐	☐	☐
Regeneration	☐	☐	☐
Conversion	☐	☐	☐
Faith	☐	☐	☐
Justification	☐	☐	☐
Sanctification	☐	☐	☐

Appendix B

Hello, Is Anyone There?

According to the George Barna Group, 25 percent of all un-churched adults in America are atheists or agnostics.[1] While atheists openly admit that it's impossible to disprove God's existence, they nonetheless assert that His existence is as improb-able as the existence of mermaids, leprechauns, and unicorns. Agnostics, on the other hand, aren't sure God exists, but are open to the possibility.[2] Therefore, if we are to be women who love God with our hearts *and* our minds, it is essential that we are able to defend God's existence to our atheistic and agnostic friends and family or any others God puts in our path.

While the cosmological, teleological, anthropological, and moral arguments are the ones most commonly used by theologians and Christian apologists to defend God's existence, I'm going to equip you to defend God's existence using a simpler approach—one that combines several approaches and uses two issues atheists and agnos-tics hold dear to their hearts—the field of science and the universe.

When speaking with a skeptic, it's important to keep in mind that we can't prove God exists with 100 percent certainty. Instead, the best we can do is to demonstrate that it is *more rational* to believe that God exists than that He doesn't exist. Therefore, this is precisely what we must tell the skeptic along with the two reasons why we believe this.

The first reason is that it is the only rational position to hold in light of an important scientific finding. While some people believe that the universe is eternal, the scientific evidence strongly suggests that the universe began to exist at some point in time. In 1920, an astronomer by the name of Edwin Hubble noticed that faraway galaxies seemed to be redder than they should be, which meant that they were uniformly expanding in all directions, much like polka dots on an uninflated balloon would grow apart as the balloon was inflated with air. In their book *Philosophical Foundations for a Christian Worldview*, theologians and Christian apologists William Lane Craig and J. P. Moreland say this finding implies that the original state of the universe was once a state of "infinite density," where all mass, energy, space, and time were contained in "a single mathematical point" from which the universe has been expanding ever since.[3] Hubble's discovery is known as the *Big Bang,* and its implication is significant: The universe had a beginning.

Therefore, since this scientific finding strongly suggests that the universe had a beginning, it logically follows that something other than itself brought it into existence. Believing that the universe popped into existence out of nothing is an irrational position to hold. If I told my friend that my piano popped into existence in my living room one day, she would disbelieve my claim as well as question my sanity because finite entities can't create themselves. Therefore, because the Big Bang suggests that the universe had a beginning, and because common sense tells us that something other than itself had to have caused it to come into existence, it also logically follows that what caused it to come into existence must have been an eternal, personal being that philosophers call the "uncaused cause." Why must this being be both personal and eternal?

Because finite things that exist in the world only exist because of choices made by other personal beings, like you and me. The only reason we are here is because our parents chose to bring us into existence or chose to engage in an act that could result in our existence. We did not create ourselves. Likewise, the only way the universe could have come into existence is if a personal being consciously chose to bring it into existence.

This being must also be eternal because if it wasn't, it would have had to create itself at some point in time. But as we have seen, this is impossible. Finite beings cannot create themselves. Someone else has to create them. For this reason, the being that created the universe must be eternal.

Thus, the question we need to ask ourselves is "Who is this personal, eternal being?" The Bible tells us it is the God Christians worship. Indeed, it is more rational to believe that God exists and created the universe than to believe that He doesn't exist and that the universe popped into existence out of nothing.

The second reason is that it is the only rational position to hold in light of the complex nature of the universe. Scientists are convinced that the conditions and composition of planet earth need to be exactly what they are in order for life on earth to be possible. For instance, the distance between the earth and the sun is such that if the earth were any closer to the sun, it would be too hot to sustain life. If it were farther away from the sun, it would be too cold to sustain life. The same is true of the composition of the earth's atmosphere. The earth's atmosphere is made up of just the right ratios of nitrogen, oxygen, and other gases in order to sustain life. If it had a higher ratio of carbon dioxide, for instance, and a lower ratio of nitrogen and other gases like Mars has, it wouldn't be able to sustain life. Again, the question we have to ask ourselves is "What could have created such a complex universe?" The answer lies in experience.

Experience has taught us that when we see something with a complex design, we immediately assume that it was created by an intelligent being. We intuitively know that things with complex designs cannot be the result of natural causes or chance acts. For instance, when I look at the design of a piano and see that it contains over 200 strings differing in length and width, which, when struck by hammers triggered by keys, produce unique sounds, I immediately infer from its complex design that it was created by an intelligent being. Common sense tells me that it is irrational to believe that when a west wind blew, scraps of wood, metal, and ivory shaped themselves into the exact dimensions needed to make up the components of a piano and then somehow assembled themselves into the configuration of said instrument.

Experience has also taught us that the more complex the design of something, the more intelligent the being who created it. If I were to find a contraption made out of paper clips, rubber bands, and batteries with a sticker on it that said "Time Machine," I would infer from its primitive design that it was the product of a small child, like my son when he was seven. However, if I were to find a painting of a man's face that so realistically captured the suffering we all sometimes feel living in a broken world, I would immediately infer from its design that it was the product of a professional artist, like Rembrandt.

When we apply our two life lessons to the mind-boggling complexity of the universe, the only rational conclusion to draw is that the universe was created by a supremely intelligent being. It is irrational to believe that it could have come into existence by random forces. Therefore, because of the highly complex design of the universe, and because entities with complex designs always imply a supremely intelligent designer, it logically follows that there was a supremely intelligent designer behind the universe's complex design. Once again, the question we need to ask ourselves is "Who could this intelligent being be?" Again, the Bible tells us that it is the God of the Bible, for He is the only being intelligent enough (and powerful enough) to have created it. This is the more rational position to hold. Believing that God doesn't exist, and that a life-sustaining universe happened by random acts or natural causes, is an irrational position.

Atheists assert that it is irrational to believe God exists. Agnostics say they can't be sure, but are open to the possibility. As we have seen, all a thinking person needs to do is examine two pieces of scientific evidence to determine which position is more rational. Consequently, as women who love God with our hearts *and* our minds, the question we need to ask the atheist or agnostic with whom we are speaking is "Which position do you want to hold, the rational position or the irrational position?" The decision is up to them.

Appendix C

Additional Logic Resources

A Concise Introduction to Logic by Patrick J. Hurley, 10th edition, Stamford, CT: Cengage Learning, 2015.

Logic Demystified by Tony Boutelle and Stan Gibilisco, New York: The McGraw-Hill Companies, Inc., 2011.

Logic Made Easy: How to Know When Language Deceives You by Deborah J. Bennett, New York: W. W. Norton & Company Inc., 2004.

Glossary of Technical Terms

abductive. Arguments that seek to find the best explanation for an event or sequence of facts.

agnostic. Suspends judgment on whether or not God exists. Concludes one cannot know.

analogy. Making a comparison of two things similar in structure for making a clarification.

animism. Deifying parts of nature like water, air, mountains, trees, and ocean. It's different from pantheism in that pantheism asserts everything in nature is God. Animism only asserts that parts of nature are God, which means that other parts of nature are not.

anthropic principle. The universe is finely tuned so that human life can live in it.

anti-supernaturalism. All supernatural explanations are rejected *a priori* (beforehand).

apologetics. Rational defense for the truth-claims of Christianity.

a posteriori. Conclusions drawn from experience.

a priori. Conclusions known prior to experience.

atheism. The belief that no god of any kind exists.

begging the question. Assuming the conclusion to be true by including it in the argument as one of its premises.

canon. The officially accepted books of Scripture.

cosmology. The study of the structure and development of the universe. It is derived from the Greek word *kosmos*, which means "orderly arrangement," or "world."

credibility. Something worthy of belief or confidence.

credulity. A disposition to believe too easily.

cultural assumptions. A premise or belief that is assumed to be true in one culture, but is not accepted in another culture.

culture wars. Expressions commonly used to express the polarized political battles over issues such as abortion, euthanasia, homosexuality, and the separation between church and state.

Darwinian Evolution. A theory that asserts that complex life forms developed from primitive life forms through natural selection, sexual selection, and/or genetic drift.

Dead Sea Scrolls. Forty thousand inscribed fragments of biblical writings, Old Testament commentaries, and other theological and social works discovered in the Qumran Caves in Israel in 1947.

deductive reasoning. Drawing specific conclusions that logically follow from established premises and known facts.

deism. The belief that a personal God exists and created the universe, but never intervenes in the world's affairs.

doctrine. A teaching that a person doesn't have to necessarily believe. Despite what some people think, the words *doctrine* and *dogma* are not synonyms. Doctrines are teachings that a person may or may not be required to believe. Dogma, on the other hand, must be believed in order to be associated with a certain theological system.

dogma. Authoritative teachings that are presented as absolute truth.

empirical. Provable by observation or experiment.

enlightenment. A philosophical movement of the eighteenth century that emphasized rationalism and encouraged skepticism about any belief that could not be proven rationally.

entropy. The measure of the amount of energy no longer able to be converted to work. Energy can be transformed from one form to another and only in one direction. For example, coal can be burned for fuel, but once it is ashes, the ashes cannot be burned for fuel.

epistemology. The branch of philosophy concerned with the nature and span of knowledge. It questions what knowledge is, how knowledge is acquired, and the extent to which something can be known.

existential questions. Questions about the meaning and purpose of life, such as "Who am I?" "What am I?" "Where am I?" "How did I get here?" "What should I consider to be important in life?" and "How am I to understand the direction and history of life?"

Ex Deo. Out of God.

Ex nihilo. Out of nothing.

fallacy. A formal or informal error in reasoning. Formal fallacies break the rules of logic. Informal fallacies divert attention away from the issue being discussed, use words or emphasize them in an ambiguous way, or fail to establish their conclusions because of poor logical structure.

general revelation. God's revelation of himself to mankind through the created world.

gnosticism. A heresy that pursued salvation through obtaining hidden knowledge and mystical experiences rather than through the revealed Word of God. It started during the early church and is once again emerging in the twenty-first century.

god of the gaps. The tendency to attribute anything we cannot explain scientifically to God.

heresy. A departure from the accepted teaching in the Christian faith, or any teaching that distorts Scripture.

humanism. The view that man is the measure of all things. In particular, man takes the place of God as the anchor for moral values. In addition, moral duties are determined by what promotes human success.

idealism. Denying the reality of nature.

immanent. Present in the natural world.

inductive reasoning. Observing patterns and using them to make generalizations, or drawing inferences from the information we have.

inerrancy. Without error.

inference. A logical conclusion derived from premises known to be true. Deductive reasoning is used to find the conclusion.

karma. A belief that states that humans are only released from the consequences of their evil actions in past lives by suffering in this life.

Law of Excluded Middle. A Law of Thought that states that a statement must either be true or false, and excludes the possibility of the truth falling somewhere in the middle.

Law of Identity. A Law of Thought that states that a thing is what it is.

Law of Noncontradiction. A Law of Thought that states that two statements cannot be true and false at the same time and in the same sense.

logical equivalence. Two statements are logically equivalent when they have the same truth values. Both are either true or false.

Masoretic text. The complete Hebrew manuscript of the Old Testament relied upon by Jews and Christians for centuries, which date back to the ninth century AD.

materialism. The view that all reality is ultimately matter or physical "stuff" in the universe.

maya. A doctrine of Hinduism that states that a person's senses are inundated with false knowledge. It usually applies to the world and reality.

metanarrative. A grand or all-encompassing story that acts as a comprehensive explanation for everything. The metanarrative explains the narratives. It's the master idea.

metaphysics. The branch of philosophy devoted to exploring questions about the nature of ultimate reality. It explores the nature of existence, the nature of time and space, the relation between mind and body, the reality of abstract objects, and the existence of God.

methodological naturalism. The philosophical view that asserts that scientific research should be limited to looking to only natural causes. Supernatural explanations are excluded *a priori* (beforehand). It's the view that science isn't science if it considers God's creative activity in the world.

methodological reductionism. Understands the whole of something by analyzing its parts.

modernism. The period in history from the Enlightenment (seventeenth and eighteenth centuries) through the late twentieth century, which holds the philosophical view that truth, meaning, and purpose are found in man, nature, and science.

modus ponens. A valid form of argument that affirms the antecedent (P). If P, then Q. P. Therefore, Q.

modus tollens. A valid form of argument that denies the consequent (Q). If P, then Q. Not Q. Therefore, not P.

monism. The metaphysical view that all reality is one. It rejects the idea that reality has two or more distinct realities.

monotheistic. The belief that there is only one God.

mutually exclusive. Two things that cannot be true at the same time.

naturalism. The belief that only the natural world exists. It doesn't believe the supernatural realm exists (God, angels, demons, and an immaterial soul).

nominalism. The philosophical view that denies the existence of universal objects or entities (or abstract entities), but affirms the existence of particular objects or entities (or concrete entities).

objective. Something is objective if it's real or true, independent of a person's opinion about it.

Old Earth Creationists. Christians who believe that God created the universe and agree with mainstream scientific estimates of the age of the earth.

219

ontological reductionism. The belief that everything that exists is made from a small number of basic substances that behave in regular ways.

ontology. The philosophical study of the nature of being, existence, or reality, and the basic categories of being and their relations.

panentheism. The idea that "all is God."

particularism. The view that salvation comes through only one religion.

philosophical skepticism. An approach that requires that all information be well supported by evidence.

physicalism. The view that man is comprised of one substance, a material body.

plenary inspiration. The view that all of Scripture is inspired by God, not just part of it.

pluralism. The view that salvation can come through different religions.

positivism. A philosophy developed in the nineteenth century by Auguste Comte that teaches that the only kind of real progress is progress made through science.

postmodernism. Both a period in history and a philosophical movement. It began toward the end of the '90s and is the view that there is no objective standard for truth, meaning, and purpose.

pragmatist. A person who believes that an idea or proposition is true if it works in the real world.

premise. The steps of an argument that lead to the conclusion.

premodernism. The period in history before the seventeenth century that holds the philosophical view that truth, meaning, and purpose is found in God.

proof. A sequence of steps that leads to an indisputable conclusion.

purpose. The goal or reason for something.

Qumran. An ancient village on the northwest shore of the Dead Sea where the Dead Sea Scrolls were discovered in 1947.

rationalism. The view that humans know what they know by their reason or minds alone.

rational argumentation. A line of reasoning given to demonstrate the truth or falsehood of something.

red herring. Diverting someone's attention away from the real issue by leading them down a different and secondary path.

reductio ad absurdum. A form of argument that proves a statement by demonstrating that its opposite is absurd.

relativism. The view that there is no objective, universal, transcendent standard for truth.

relativist. A person who believes that truth is relative rather than absolute.

religious imperialism. Spreading religious conviction to others through oppressive means.

scientism. The worldview that true knowledge can only be obtained scientifically.

scientific naturalism. The view that the universe and everything in it should be investigated and understood through the natural world alone.

Second Law of Thermodynamics. A closed system (a physical system that does not allow transfers of any kind like mass in or out of the system) will inevitably move toward thermodynamic equilibrium (heat death) through the loss of heat (entropy). This law shows that the universe is running out of usable energy.

secularism. A worldview that allows no room for the supernatural, such as miracles, divine revelation, God, angels, demons, and immaterial souls.

Septuagint. The first Greek translation of the Hebrew Old Testament, which dates from the third century BC.

skepticism. An attitude of doubt about facts, opinions, beliefs, and anything asserted as truth.

slippery slope. Asserting a false cause or a cause that lacks enough reason that sets off a chain reaction or domino effect.

Sola Scriptura. The view that the Christian's authoritative source is the Bible and the Bible alone.

solipsism. The view that the self is the only reality that can be known.

special revelation. The Bible is the means through which God reveals himself to humans about himself, humans, the world, and His plan for man's salvation.

straw man. Distorting another person's argument and then attacking the distorted view, which isn't the real argument.

subjective. A matter of personal opinion. The statement, "Chocolate tastes better than vanilla," is an example.

substance dualism. The view that man is comprised of two substances: a material body and an immaterial soul.

tautology. A self-supporting statement that is always necessarily true because of the way it is structured.

totalitarian. Controlled by a single party or dictator.

transcendent. Above and independent of the material universe.

Two Books Theory. God reveals himself to mankind through two books: the book of the world (General Revelation) and the Bible (Special Revelation).

value. What a person decides is good and evil and right and wrong.

verbal inspiration. The very words in the Bible are inspired by God, not only the ideas or themes.

worldview. A conceptual framework for interpreting reality. How one sees the world at large.

Young Earth Creationists. Christians who believe that God created the universe in six consecutive days (twenty-four hours in a day) within the last 6,000 to 10,000 years.

Patty Houser (MA, Christian Apologetics, Biola University) is the director of Women's Ministries for Solid Reasons and is a national conference speaker and teacher who equips women to share and defend their faith in language women best understand: woman to woman. She lives with her husband and son in Burke, Virginia. Learn more at www.pattyhouser.com.